When Hope Is Lost

By

Mosey Stuart

STUDIO OF BOOKS
THE SPACE FOR YOUR MESSAGE

Studio of Books LLC
5900 Balcones Drive Suite 100
Austin, Texas 78731
www.studioofbooks.org
Hotline: (254) 800-1183

Ordering Information:
Special discounts are available on quantity purchases by corporations, associations, and others. For details, contact the publisher at the address above.

Printed in the United States of America.

ISBN-13: Softcover   978-1-968491-69-7
        Hardback: 978-1-968491-70-3
        Ebook   978-1-968491-71-0

Library of Congress Control Number: 2025918177

Dedication

This book is dedicated to my children, whom I love dearly. You may not all be mine in blood, but you are most definitely mine in heart and in spirit, and I am proud of you all. I persevered through this life to teach you from my mistakes, to give you more than I had, to lift and encourage you, and to give you hope. Never give up on yourself and keep dreaming.

Acknowledgments

To my parents, siblings, and friends who stuck with me through the most challenging times; you picked me up, carried me, encouraged me, and pushed me to keep going. Thank you for the endless prayers, the wisdom you shared, and the compassion you showed me. Most of all, thank you for never giving up on me and helping to keep hope.

Contents

Chapter 1:

YOU'RE MAKING HISTORY

History can be defined in many ways, but what defines *your* history? If you consider the dictionary's definition of history, 'the whole series of past events connected with someone or something', it opens the door to consider an extensive past reality. One could say, "you are a sum of your past events". However, our past events are not exclusively caused by us as individuals, but by every person, and every circumstance or situation involving us both directly, and indirectly.

Everything you do and everything that happens to you is a part of your history, and that history is constantly being compounded. When you understand that everything you do is making history, perhaps that changes the way you approach your life, your relationships, and your future.

History is a valuable tool that we have used, and continue to use, in all areas of life, throughout our entire existence. From the beginning of time, however that falls into your personal beliefs, we have used history as a learning tool. It is full of the experiences and events that tell us where we came from, how we came to be, what works, what doesn't, and what is safe; it teaches us right from wrong.

Everything you know today is a result of history. Somebody had to experience it, or it had to happen, in order for it to *become* history. Thankfully, we don't have to experience all of the same events in history to benefit from the learning, the sacrifice, and the freedom we now have and understand. History also creates for us a foundation of comparison. It details specific ideas and events that we can use to predict future events, such as weather and business strategies, or used as a comparison tool to set or measure standards or progress. It's our common point of reference for everything we make decisions about.

When a meteorologist forecasts the weather, they use history to try to provide a more accurate prediction. Similarly, marketing companies make predictions based on past sales and demographics, and business executives make large business decisions based on past experience, whether their own personal experience or in combination with the experiences of others. As we progress through grade school and our higher education, we take tests based on and weighed against the standards of progress that were determined through the historical performance of other students. In our relationships we use our previous experience, or history, of those around us to compare as a point of reference to what we expect comes next and when. If someone doesn't meet our standards of progress, we often make the decision to leave that relationship in search of one that meets our historically based standards. We all use history to shape our everyday activities.

When you are very young you experience everything for the first time. You learn what 'hot' means, you learn the word 'no', you learn what is good, what is bad. Your parents likely taught you these things based on their own history, the things they learned through past experiences. As you grew older, you learned how to clean, how to cook, and how to make friends. When you were testing the waters and learning to date, you either based your actions on history or created a history by taking your own actions. You eventually grew up and got a job, started a business, explored the world, had a family, stayed single, etc. Everybody has a different experience for each of these situations, but they all work together to make our unique and individual history.

What we don't spend enough time doing is reviewing our own history; not dwelling on the past but looking back to understand what happened. Determining if the things in our past are worth repeating or letting go of, whether a decision was good or bad, and whether a relationship was healthy or not is very valuable. Knowing that everything you do is creating your history, why would you just ignore the history you have already made as if it had no bearing on your future? There are many ways to review your own history, but if you're afraid of it or ashamed of it, you may want to seek out professional guidance to sort through your past.

Having a history you're not proud of doesn't make you broken. There's nothing wrong with you; it's just yours. You have a decision now to look at that past and decide what is worth taking into the future, and what is ok to leave behind. You can learn from your history. That is what it's there for. It is the foundation on which your entire future life is built. If you were going to build a house and you put down a strong foundation, but extending from that strong foundation was a less reliable, weaker foundation, would you still build out? Of course not! You would build *up* rather than out. Some of us don't have a lot of good foundation to build our lives on and that's ok. Some of us were meant to build up, and some of us were meant to build out. Let time wash away the weaker foundation so that what is left is the strength of a positive and healthy future.

Our history can define us as a person but we must also understand that as a unique and individual person, we can define our history. When you wake up in the morning your first thought probably isn't, "what will I put in my history today?". That might sound like a silly thought but it is just a different way to approach your day. It will affect your attitude, your motivation, and your daily decisions. Creating history means you're moving forward because you can't live in the past and simultaneously create a new one. Many of us have a past, or "history", that we maybe don't like, are ashamed of, or even are afraid of. That is what makes that question so empowering. You're making history with every decision, every breath. If you can make your history great, it will extend beyond your living years. It's called a legacy. Let your history become a legacy.

What will you define in your history?

Chapter 2:

YOU ARE NOT ALONE

Although we all have our own unique life experiences, there are similarities between those experiences and what other people experience as well. In fact, in most cases, it might be safe to assume that when we experience something, whether good or bad, we are neither the first nor the last to have that experience. Knowing that you're not alone is comforting, but only helpful if you're willing to put down your guard enough to get to know the people around you. Somebody somewhere has dealt with your history in their own way. It is up to you to take initiative to find them because they aren't usually looking for you. Don't let naivety cause you loneliness. You can be lonely if you're happy, and you can be lonely if you're sad. Sometimes all you want to do is celebrate an achievement or a personal victory with someone. You are happy because you have this accomplishment, but you are lonely because there isn't anybody to share it with. I assure you, somebody absolutely wants to celebrate with you because you're worth celebrating.

Life has a way of making us feel alone, but only if we allow it. The way our society has evolved has caused a disconnect. We are now so "connected" through electronic means and social media platforms that we no longer share the true personal connections we once had. Being connected through artificial means, other than physical interaction, creates a false reality. As people we need community. Whether we realize it or not we were created to seek out community, we strive for connection to others. The connection we now understand as normal is not necessarily artificial but it is insufficient. When you receive a 'like' or a message through a social media outlet you get the feeling of acknowledgment, which is great. Having contact with somebody or something is good, but what is missing is the genuineness of human contact.

You cannot send the same emotion through a text message, emoji, gif, etc., that you can in person talking and connecting face to face. I strongly believe people have power in their presence. Most of us know somebody that creates emotional response at the sight of them or we can feel when they enter a room. Think about your favorite actor/actress, performer, favorite relative, or even your best friend; they can all create atmosphere with their physical presence. By taking away the need for physical presence to have interactions, it becomes so easy to feel alone. "Why didn't they text me back?" "Why isn't anybody commenting on my post?" "Nobody sends me funny messages." It is easy to be excluded from social groups, develop personal insecurities, and become depressed solely based on the electronic interaction, or lack thereof, between peers.

Social platforms are not a bad thing. In fact, they are potentially a great resource to be able to find and connect with others who relate to us that we otherwise would never have known. These methods are already being used to form 'groups' and 'followings' for people with similar interests and life experiences. Use these resources! The old-fashioned way of meeting people still works and it is still effective, but the diversity and speed at which new connections can now happen are dramatically increased with electronic communication. In seconds, you can be connected to people who have experienced similar losses, addictions, and separations, as well as achieved similar victories, reached new goals, and people who are also trying to make a positive difference in the world.

Let's set aside social media for a minute and look at the people immediately surrounding us, our family and our closest friends. These are people we talk to very regularly, people who ensure that we are never left to be alone. We don't really have to go looking for them because they're usually seeking us out or already present in our daily life. You might think, "I have done something so horrible that nobody could ever want to be around me". That is not true, and you are not alone. Somebody close to you will always be there; it may not always be the same person, but somebody wants to be there for you so you are not alone. We don't have perfect families, and we don't have perfect friends, but we have them. If your life has gone in a direction that none of those people who were once close to you are still around, there is still somebody who wants to be there for you. When you need to celebrate something and you've burned all your bridges in the past, there is still somebody who wants to share in your victory. It is not always easy but you don't ever have to be alone, especially when it comes to life circumstances.

Feeling alone can be a dangerous feeling. It can lead to self-isolation, fear, anxiety, depression, and in some cases, suicide. What propels a person into loneliness varies, but one contributing factor is believing you are alone because you deserve to be. Perhaps you made a very bad decision, something nobody else knows about. Knowing that you're the only person that knows what happened can make it difficult to cope. You already feel alone because you think that nobody else has done this or that no one understands your situation. It scares you to think about the consequences if the wrong person finds out what you have done or the thoughts you have had. The guilt or the shame has caused you to fall into depression, pressing you into isolation. You become alone through your own decision-making. If left to your own lonely thoughts, you might feel so trapped that the only way out is to take your own life. Besides, who could love somebody like you? That is wrong! Somebody like you is absolutely worth loving. I think sometimes, the most broken people are the ones we forget to love the most.

Maybe you did something that people wouldn't approve of, but you're not worthless. It is very likely many people feel the way you do, and plenty of people have made the same poor choices. Do you think you're the first and only person to make this bad decision? Then maybe you should be rewarded for discovering something new! The likelihood that you're the first person ever to do something wrong is unrealistic. You don't have to be alone, somebody else has done this too. There are unlimited resources, some of them anonymous if you desire, to help you share and not be alone. Please understand that this isn't to downplay the severity of some people's actions, but know that there are people out there who do not want you to be alone, regardless of the circumstance.

Loneliness causes us to believe lies that we normally wouldn't even consider. When you are surrounded by even one person who desires for you not to be alone, it is significantly easier to overcome the self told lies we often hear in loneliness. Suppose we start and learn from a young age the importance of good and positive relationships. In that case, we can prepare ourselves to make better decisions overall and, in turn, avoid some of the potential loneliness we would have otherwise experienced. And, by default, if we still make poor choices, we are not doing it alone. One person can make a difference in your life. Understanding that you don't have to be alone and that you do not deserve to be alone is crucial. When you have friends, you might still feel alone like you don't belong. Maybe you're different, maybe your hair isn't styled right, or your clothes aren't cool, or your family situation is not as affluent. None of those things are reasons you should feel you deserve to be alone.

I have had a life that has brought me through some very painful and traumatic experiences. Some of those events left long-lasting effects on my emotions, my mind, my relationships, and my life. I used to think that I was so unique in my life circumstances that nobody could have ever experienced things the way that I did. I used to think I was alone in understanding what I had been through and how that affected me and continues to affect me. The truth is, I was so wrapped up in my own trauma that I wouldn't even allow the *possibility* of someone else the opportunity to understand my psyche.

I am choosing not to write about my traumas, because that would only be boasting about the terrible things that happened in my life. I'm not sending invitations for a pity party, I'm not looking for excuses, I am not going to wear my trauma like a badge of honor. I am choosing to write about the *effects* of my trauma so that, like me, you may understand that you're not alone in what you feel or think, because you're not broken, and you're not crazy.

The first thing that I really want you to understand is that trauma is all based on perception. I am not discounting any person's perceived traumatic event, but it is important for you to know, both for yourself and for others, that what happened in your life that you perceived as trauma may not seem traumatic to someone else, and vice versa. Second, trauma affects different people in different ways, based significantly on the experiences they had growing up and the ways they learned to cope through them, as well as their personality, their age, and their level of maturity.

If I summed up all the traumatic experiences in my life, I would say that I never fully healed from any one of them completely before the next one occurred, making each experience a compounded one. This caused the perception of each event to be seen through a lens of negative magnification. This is why it is so important to be honest with yourself, and to surround yourself with people who truly care about you, people that don't need or want anything from you but just want to love you. What might not have been that bad was made worse by not being able to, or not being aware of, how to heal and recover from the previous event. This is my story. It might be yours, it might not, but if it is in any way, I hope you can understand that you're not alone.

I didn't fully notice or even see the effects of my unresolved wounds until it was far too late for my ongoing relationships. I did notice that some things about myself didn't quite feel normal, but I wasn't exactly sure why or how. I found myself cycling through the same patterns in all the relationships in my life for well over 20 years, every year compounding on the one before. I would say that the most prevalent symptom I can recall was the constant feeling of rejection. I took everything personally. If you were going to call me and you didn't, I felt rejected. If you were cheering at a sporting event where I performed and I didn't get the recognition, I felt not good enough. If I sent you a message or an email or left you a voicemail to call me back and I never got a reply, I felt rejected and unimportant. When I started dating and that person wouldn't be where they said they would be or when they said they would be there, when they changed or cancelled plans, I took it personally as if there was something wrong with me. I remember very good, close friends I would be at an event with or be waiting to talk to in a group setting, that if they didn't talk to me because they were in conversation with somebody else, I thought of it as just another rejection.

This thought process was, and is, dangerous. To constantly think I was not good enough was so demeaning and caused intense chronic depression and some very negative thoughts. This kind of depression can lead down a path of unhealthy coping mechanisms, often leading to unhealthy addictions. For me, I started to make decisions based on what other people were doing that I admired or envied for their popularity, or what I perceived as popularity. I saw others getting attention for something they were doing, so I did that. I didn't really care about or consider the consequences at the time because I just had this innate desire to fit in and feel accepted. I was living in a broken reality.

This rejection carried into relationships and caused problems in my ability to make choices that were healthy for me. I would lower my standards and be more accepting of things that I maybe shouldn't have, or normally wouldn't have, had I dealt with the emotional and psychological aspects of healing from my life's traumas. This meant that every person I was in a relationship with had to deal with me from a foundation of brokenness. That is a difficult burden to place on anyone, especially somebody that you are pursuing long-term goals with, and it is very straining on any relationship. Typically, the other person doesn't understand why you are acting the way you do, or know what you have been through. They don't consider your broken foundation as the reason you are inappropriate, and they just see you as rude, aggressive, immature, or even dangerous. They usually don't stick around long enough to help you and, when they do, it is still too overwhelming for most and they end up leaving anyway. This process further enhances feelings of rejection and causes even more reinforced depression. I found myself struggling just to pass the days, feeling constantly hopeless and not ever good enough.

When I did manage to find some peace or something good, it was short-lived, and I ended up right back under the heavy blanket of depression. Feeling constantly rejected also put my emotions out of whack. I was so into my own world of thought and depression, I experienced uncharacteristic anger and short temperament. The smallest thing would set me off, often something insignificant. I would not normally react this way but because my brain was so constantly overwhelmed, I could only react out of anger as a defense mechanism. I was fighting myself, and I didn't even know *why* most of the time. I felt like nobody else understood me. I mean, honestly, I didn't even understand myself, so I wouldn't have expected anyone else to. I can remember really dumb things that set me off, like after putting my contacts in and they made my eyes itch, I would get angry and just scream out loud in overwhelming frustration. I remember while reaching for a glass and, whether it was full or empty, it would tip over, and I would react with the same helpless outburst. If I lost a signal on a phone call, I was just ready to throw my phone, and sometimes I did.

I could keep my explosive anger under control, but not when I was alone. When I was around other people I fought it and forced myself to behave, which only bottled it up for later when I was alone and I would let it all out. At one point, well more than once, I brought up my concerns of anger to different psychologists and psychiatrists. One of them made the following statement to me that I remember to this day any time I am feeling upset, "why does that make you so angry?". Such a simple question, but difficult to come up with that thinking on my own because of my elevated mental state of unresolved trauma.

Why was I so angry? Why did these silly little things set me off to the point of explosive behavior? I didn't have the answer then, and I am not sure I have the answer now, but my answer is going to be different than yours. The point of the question is to slow down and focus enough to self-reflect. Take time to look at your situation and think about how you would like to respond instead of how you have been reacting. This is going to take some time to change or reprogram your brain to process this way, but it will begin to help over time.

Time alone isn't the answer because it is going to take effort from you to seek help as well as work on yourself. No matter how bad your situation is or has been, there is *somebody* out there who has had the same or very similar experiences. It really helped me to meet people and have conversations about our similar traumatic experiences and how we have been able to cope or how we have suffered. I felt so much more at peace to know that there really was someone else that felt the same way I did, because

I felt so extreme that I couldn't imagine somebody else going through the same process. In fact, not only were they coping with the same struggles, but they had found someone to be by their side in the process, which gives me hope in believing there really is someone out there who is capable and willing to fight alongside me in my battles to victory over my traumatic past.

There are fortifying benefits to understanding you're not alone. The way you think becomes different, the confidence you have in yourself is greater, your relationships are healthier, and your outlook on life tends to be more positive. Knowing that there is somebody who wants to support you in your life can give you the motivation and courage to chase your dreams and accomplish great things. It can create feelings of belonging and being loved. It is important that you feel wanted, that you feel somebody loves you. When you understand that you're not alone, it can encourage you to go out of your way to make sure somebody else doesn't feel alone. If we all pitch in just a little, we could make the communities we live in a much happier place.

Chapter 3:

IDENTITY THEFT

When you hear the words, "identity theft", do you think happy, positive thoughts? Probably not. They might even stir up some pretty aggressive emotions. Maybe you have been a victim of identity theft yourself. It can leave you feeling vulnerable, violated, angry, paranoid, and a variety of other emotions. Somebody didn't just steal something *from* you, they stole you! You are entitled to feel all of those things and more. When you are a victim of identity theft, you aren't just robbed of stuff; you are robbed of yourself. Somebody is pretending to be you, and not in a flattering way. The financial damage, annually, caused by identity theft is in the billions! That is an incredible loss! As a result we, as consumers, spend our hard-earned money to keep that theft from happening. If it does happen, we like to believe that our insurance gives us assurance that everything will be ok. But what about our actual identity?

Let's start with the word "identity". Identity is defined as "the distinguishing character or personality of an individual". There is something that distinguishes you from everyone else out there, something that makes you identifiably you. What is it? How is it? In the bible, it is written that, "Before I formed you in the womb, I knew you...". This idea doesn't take away from our individuality. In fact, it necessarily adds to it. These words give us the promise that we were created for something specific, to be *someone* specific. The fact that we don't just exist by chance or just for the mere fact of existing means that we have the opportunity to have an identity. This is life changing! Your life has a purpose! Your purpose it to be somebody, not just anybody, but to be *you*. Your daily decisions make you into the person you are, and your decisions are based on your personality.

Now, what can you do to understand yourself? There must be a process to understand your identity or, even before that, to *learn* your identity. At some point in your life, you may experience an "identity crisis". This happened to me. I thought it was just because the period of my life I was going through was a real struggle but it turns out, in retrospect, I was living in an identity crisis because I had not yet discovered my true identity. Maybe this sounds like you but, if not, allow me still to dive a little deeper into this revelation. Not knowing my true identity was no big deal when I didn't know what

I didn't know, but I still had an emotional longing to be somebody. As I grew up I learned behavioral traits like most children, from my parents, siblings, and close friends. My personality directly reflected the people I was spending the most time around. This makes complete sense when you think about it. Even as an adult, it is said that you are a combination of the five people you spend the most time with. But as you are a child learning the process of becoming a person and developing a character or personality, you don't really understand right from wrong. That is also another learned trait. Morals are often developed relative to a person's surroundings that they are familiar with.

As I learned new personality traits, some of them felt normal and some of them felt weird, like they just didn't fit "me". This, I believe, is because some of the personality traits I was learning were aligning with a preprogrammed personality for me, and others were not. This didn't make them wrong, just not right for me. We all know somebody that is naturally quiet and introverted, and we do not expect them to be loud and outspoken or even to be comfortable stepping out. The same applied in reverse, as the loud and outspoken individual is often jittery with anticipation when demanded to be still. There are different personalities and different identities that we are pre-programmed with, and as we grow up we discover what fits with us individually. Imagine the children's toy that is a box with shaped holes cut into it, with matching pieces to fit inside the corresponding holes. The objective of the child is to determine which shaped piece fits into the correctly shaped holes.

This process is much like the determination and understanding of our individual identity. We cannot force a personality, or shape, into the hole, or person, in which it does not fit or belong. Attempting to do this creates frustration and it will not work, regardless of how many times you try. If we can begin to identify what fits into our personality, we begin to understand ourselves. But what if we start to put somebody else's shapes into our box? The right shapes will fit, but they're not ours.

When you begin to identify with the personality traits of people around you, you find common ground, and when you have common ground, you have a basis for friendship. Sometimes, that common ground becomes an idolatrous platform, and we begin to very strongly envy that person for their personality. Even so much that we begin to be like them, we begin to put their shapes into our own box. We "steal" their identity. This can be easy to do because we enjoy the presence of certain people so much that we think if we just become them, everybody will like us just as much. This thought process is dangerous because we weren't wired to handle being anybody but ourselves. When we steal somebody else's identity we forget about who we are, and we can no longer make decisions with our own thought processes. We must wait for our example to do something so we can imitate it. Imitation is thought to be the greatest form of flattery; however, it is also the easiest way to lose your own identity.

When you seek the friendship of another you look for common traits, but if you looked for all the exact same traits, you would never have any friends. There is only one of you, and one of them, and so on. It is ok to honor personality traits that we enjoy and appreciate in other people and even to adapt some of them for ourselves. It is not ok to try to become somebody else simply by copying everything they are, and to do so in order to leave your own identity behind. It is good and healthy to have friendships with contrasting personalities. These relationships teach us to expand our thinking and understanding of people beyond what we can do on our own. So, how do you get your shapes put into your box? By understanding you were created for a unique, individual purpose and acknowledging your own strengths and weaknesses in your personality. It is going to take time and, in some cases, a lifetime. As I stated previously, I didn't know what I didn't know.

I discovered my identity crisis at a time in my life when there was such chaos and confusion that I fell into a deep pit of depression and realized, "I don't even know who I really am". I had tried so tirelessly to fit in throughout my childhood, but I didn't realize or understand that my "fitting in" was just me stealing everyone else's identity one personality trait at a time, whether-or-not it fit. You could say that I was trying to put someone else's star shape into my square hole, and I was getting frustrated. I wanted to fit in and be accepted for who I was, but the problem was that I wasn't ever me. I learned much later, in my adult life, that there was a reason I hadn't fit in. It wasn't because there was anything wrong with me, I wasn't broken, I just wasn't learning to be me. I wasn't developing my own identity. I was just a thief.

Unfortunately for me, it took falling into a deep hole of what I perceived as life-failure-induced depression to understand that my whole life was just me trying to be everybody else. I truly hope this isn't you, but if you are reading this and you are identifying with me, please don't stop reading. I want you to experience the full freedom of understanding who you are and that you do in fact have an incredible personality and a purposeful identity.

Through a lengthy and humbling process of digging through my past and past relationships, I began to understand that my desire for acceptance had fueled my thievery. After all, who doesn't want to be accepted? I started to unfold the major events of my childhood and young adult years, and I began to see the places where I discovered personality traits that, if I liked and felt would be accepted, I adopted them as my own. Looking back, I understand why I felt so confused. I was simply trying to be a combination of everybody rather than feeling what fit right for me. I discovered in my seemingly wholesome Christian upbringing that I still felt alone and unworthy. I was striving so hard to be *something*; I just wasn't sure what. I would pick a personality to practice for a while and then another, and another, until I had tried them all.

My problem was that I wasn't discarding anything, but rather holding onto all of them in case I might need them again at some point. I should have been determining which traits fit me, which ones came naturally, which ones *felt* natural. Nobody taught me how to do this or that it was even a real process. I didn't know what I didn't know.

As things, and people, in my life were changing, I was staying the same in a way. At least I was processing everything the same way. I was stuck, and I wasn't changing. I didn't know how to change, I just knew how to follow examples. I wasn't trying to pave my own way and it was causing me to walk further and further away from knowing my identity. As I aged into adulthood, I was as confused and lost as I had ever been. So many new personalities, so many new people, new situations, and new problems. I was struggling to create my own identity; I was struggling to be an individual, to set myself apart. I wanted to be a leader, I wanted people to follow me, but I was just a follower myself. So in the process of seeking comfort, I reverted to the personalities I knew as a child and understood. That still wasn't me; it was everybody else, except now it was what everybody else *used* to be.

I drowned myself in self-pity and depression longing for acceptance, but I was doing it to myself out of a combination of laziness and naivety. I never had somebody step in and truly teach me 'identity' or the importance of it. I had tried to fill the emptiness in my life with all the wrong things. What I was failing to realize was that I wasn't actually empty. You can't fill a full glass. I was missing the fact that I was already full. I kept trying to stick more identities into my glass, but nothing fit, nothing stuck, because my glass was already full of my identity!

I was fortunate to be in the right place at the right time (not likely a coincidence). I was really struggling with my past and my current life choices and situations. Things had not turned out the way I had hoped or planned and I felt like my world was caving in on me. This is the point I now understand as the 'climax' of my identity crisis. The idea holds true, 'the night is always darkest just before the dawn". I was having a conversation with another person who had a few more years of life experience, and they were explaining to me that my current circumstances weren't what defined me. They weren't who I was. They weren't my identity. It was in this conversation that I learned I had been the victim of identity theft, but not as one who was taken from, but one who had unknowingly taken.

I was emboldened by the reality that I was not defined by any single moment, but by all moments, and only in part; because what defined me most were my decisions 'today'. I believe I had an identity that was programmed into me, and my journey in this life was to discover and reveal to myself, through trial and error, of what that identity, what that purpose, was. I didn't need to steal another person's identity and I didn't need to borrow their purpose. The shifting of characteristics and personality traits was my sorting process to uncover for myself where I fit in to my identity. It makes sense that the activities that felt comfortable were the ones I was designed for, that the personality traits I took on naturally were for me. You see, I was meant to try on the different styles of personality, just not hold onto all of them. Who I surrounded myself with helped me to uncover or reveal my own true identity.

The more people I was able to interact with and spend time with, the more people I was able to understand, the more I revealed within myself who I was and what I knew myself to be. Imagine that everything you are, or everything you're going to be, was programmed inside of your DNA at compounded levels, and your job through life was to uncover, or excavate, as many levels as you can. How far will you dig to discover yourself? Every time you learned something new about yourself you leveled up. Your goal is to level up as much as you can, and this allows you to function in your life at a higher and higher level. Maybe at some point we all get to a level that our purpose becomes helping others understand their identity, their purpose. I had to listen to my inner man to understand what made a good fit and what made me scream inside. Sometimes we wait too long and develop bad characteristics, in which case the right thing for us may be uncomfortable, but ultimately this is why you need to surround yourself with the right people so they can guide you through the shifting puzzle of your own internal morality. Exchanging bad habits for good ones is uncomfortable, but a necessary growth pain.

My identity matches who I need to be to live out my purpose. They're beautifully intertwined, and as I began to understand my identity, my purpose became more clear. Knowing, I mean fully knowing, receiving, and believing your identity, gives you the power to overcome everything and anything life has to put in your path. It helps you to become more successful, more relatable, more compassionate, you will be able to help more people around you. You get to know yourself so well and have such confidence that you move like water through all the obstacles life throws at you. And just like water, when you hit a wall, or a dam, you can build yourself up until you flow over that obstacle, even if it takes time.

In your fullest comprehension of your own identity, you are unstoppable. Will you use your resilience to gain selfishly, or will you use it to lift others up? Water can flood a nation, or lift their ships. What will you do with *your* identity?

Chapter 4:

WHEN THE MIRROR LOOKS AT YOU

A mirror is an awesome creation. It allows us to see what other people see. It can be used to check for injury, beauty applications, training in sports, medical procedures, dentistry, etc. Mirrors can be manipulated to magnify or reduce the reflected image as well as be distorted, like what you might find at a fun carnival attraction. Whatever the application, the function is still the same; to reflect what is placed in front of it. This can be great news for some and intimidating for others because mirrors don't, and can't lie. Unmanipulated designs are the purest truth we can use for this reality. If you are lying to yourself that you're losing weight, the mirror will tell you the truth. If you are bruised, the mirror isn't going to lie to you, or for you. If you have bad form when you're lifting weights or practicing your dance routine, the mirror isn't going to correct it. The mirror won't lie to you about your acne. The mirror can seem cruel in its reflection, but it is simply displaying the truth in an extremely unfiltered and realistic way. Arguing with the mirror would be nonsense and, in turn, arguing with yourself and the truth of your own reality.

What is more awkward than standing in front of a mirror looking at yourself from head to toe? You can see all your imperfections, or perfections, whether you like it or not. But do you still only see what you want, or do you see what the mirror sees? The thing about looking at yourself in the mirror is that you are looking at yourself with judgement, contrasting and comparing everything you see with somebody or everybody else. When you look at the mirror, you see a slightly distorted version of yourself simply because when you look through your eyes, your reflection goes through your "life filter". That filter is the complex combination of your life experiences and your understanding of them. It is time to look at yourself from the mirror's perspective. What does the mirror see when it looks at you?

You can run from the truth; you might even be able to hide from it, but you can't deny it. The truth is exactly that: truth. We don't always like it, so we run or try to convince ourselves otherwise. We don't always want to look at it, so we hide. Our reflection of ourselves doesn't have to be something that destroys us, and it certainly shouldn't make us nervous. I have met many people who get very uncomfortable in front of a mirror or a camera because they're not comfortable with what they see. Unfortunately, they don't see what we see because, if they did, they would have no reason to hide and they would be happy to look in the mirror. The mirror allows us to look at ourselves from an outside perspective, it helps us to see things we wouldn't otherwise be able to see. Just try to look at your chin or your forehead. Everybody else can see those things, and maybe it's the first thing they notice about you, but you can't see it on your own. You wouldn't know anything was wrong unless somebody told you. This is the problem. We don't always have somebody willing to tell us. How can you know there's something wrong with the things you can't see unless somebody tells you?

Now, to take it a step further, you would never know what you looked like if you didn't have a mirror. Your looks help you understand and determine who you are, or can help you show others who you are. It helps to create an identity if you can see what other people are looking at. The mirror allows you to modify and adjust your physical appearance to align with your learned or developed identity. It can be tempting to use the ability to see your reflection to hide yourself or to mold yourself after somebody else's identity. Don't use this tool to steal somebody's identity. Use it to help you create and understand your own.

Understanding the truth about your life and who you are will help you to see what the mirror sees. You have a purposeful identity and a great and unique personality, so don't try to hide it. Let your reflection be equally real from this side of the mirror. It doesn't matter where you came from or even where you are; when you look in a mirror anywhere in the world, you see the same thing every time. It doesn't matter what language you speak, what color you are, or what you've done; your reflection is always going to be *you* at that very moment.

The most incredible thing about the mirror is that when it looks at you it doesn't see the past, it doesn't see what you've done or where you've been; it sees who you are right now. Nothing else matters. Can you see *that* when you look in your mirror? Can you see 'you right now'? Stop looking at yourself through your life filter and just see yourself in the moment. You are who you are, not who you *were*. Even if your past is incredibly amazing, it is still gone; it is no longer "now". When you look in the mirror, imagine you are in the mirror, and your reflection is looking at you. You get to be the truth of what the mirror sees. Would your mirror tell you that you are fat? You're ugly? You're not good enough? You're a failure? Or you're useless? Of course not, so don't say that to yourself because that doesn't reflect the truth. Your reflection should empower and encourage you. When you see yourself, be proud that you know the truth, and that truth will set you free.

I learned about my true identity, and I no longer felt the pressure of being somebody because I learned that I was already me. I was free from the standards of society, free from the captivity of imitation. I had finally reached a point where I could breathe and make decisions based on myself, who I was, and how I wanted to enhance my own personality. I had finally learned to be proud that I was different because different was me. It didn't matter anymore what other people did and *who* they were. I had discovered my own personality.

Growing up, I never really spent much time getting ready to go anywhere because my hair style was short and simple and, as a boy, there really wasn't much to do. Most of the time I spent in front of the mirror was brushing my teeth. I distinctly remember each time I brushed my teeth and looked at myself I felt weird, and I got really giggly. That never really made sense to me, and I thought it was weird and a little embarrassing to look at myself. But it wasn't just my mirror at home or when I brushed my teeth; it was every mirror, everywhere. I guess the biggest thing was that I didn't know what I was supposed to do when I looked in the mirror. All I knew was what I saw in the movies. Nobody really talks about mirror etiquette, if there is such a thing. What do you say when you look in the mirror, or should you say anything at all? Are you supposed to do, or not do, certain things? How should it feel to look at yourself?

What really got me confused was when I stood in front of the mirror looking at myself and somebody else was looking in the mirror too. I wasn't sure if I should look at myself or at them, or neither. I felt really insecure because what I saw in the mirror was not what I thought I was supposed to see. I thought I should look a certain way and I knew I didn't. Well, I thought I knew. What is important to know about that is; it doesn't matter what someone else's reflection is because no matter what someone else sees, your reflection is always going to be you. I would have liked to have learned many years ago what the mirror saw when I looked at it. I kept trying to see somebody else when I looked in the mirror, which is why I was never satisfied and always embarrassed and uneasy. Of course I felt silly when I looked in the mirror because it was telling me the truth, and I was trying to argue with it. I might as well have just closed my eyes and looked at a rock. It would have been equally productive for my identity.

After learning the truth of my identity, I had the opportunity to reinforce my new-found understanding of my personality and strengthen my self-view. I began working at a job where I was forced to look at myself constantly, from every angle. I was surrounded by head-to-toe mirrors. I knew who I was now, but I still hadn't been comfortable looking at it. If you've ever been in a bridal shop, then you know what I am talking about when I say surrounded from every angle. The longer I worked in this position the more I looked at myself, and the more I looked at myself, the more I transitioned from judgement to admiration and acceptance. I learned to be proud of who I had been and appreciate what it took to be right where I was, and who I was in that moment.

I knew who I was on the inside, and I wanted the outside to match. As I looked at myself every day from every angle for 8 hours, I discovered that the outside already matched the inside; it was just a process to let those meld together in my own brain. Once I accepted the fact that I was the person the mirror saw me to be, that

I didn't have to look for somebody else in my reflection, my confidence skyrocketed! I was so comfortable looking in the mirror at who I knew I was that I began to help other people see themselves as the mirror saw them.

If you look in the mirror and you see somebody else, that's not a mirror. It is just a window. You can no longer allow yourself to be held captive by pursuing a reflection or identity that is not your own. Don't go window shopping for a personality. You've already got one staring back at you. It is time to embrace your reflection and see yourself the way the mirror does. When you look in the mirror, you see who you want. When the mirror looks at you, it sees who you are, it sees your true identity.

Chapter 5:

GETTING OLDER DOESN'T MEAN GROWING UP

We all get older, that's inevitable, but it doesn't mean we have grown up. In fact, you very likely know someone who has gotten older but hasn't grown up. Aging is a physical process that happens to everyone but growing up is a psychological thing. We often learn to "grow up" as we get older, but sometimes we get stuck along the way. Some of us will experience trauma that keeps us from growing up as we get older, in a sort of mentally protective process, and others stay childish, often because it is easier or safer. After all, it is familiar. Growing up can be scary due to the nature of the unknown, or because of what we *do* know and have learned about other people we have seen getting older and growing up. Growing up is a process you get to control if you choose, and it can be very fulfilling if you do it to suit your personality.

As children, we spend countless hours daydreaming about growing up and getting older so we can have and do the things we feel restricted from. On the other hand, once we have grown up we spend about as much time wishing we could go back and be a child again. This is where the conflict begins. As people, we tend to have a desire for the things we don't, and often cannot, have. In the context of growing up, this can cause someone to get stuck somewhere in-between and cause incredible confusion, ultimately leading to their own self-destruction, whether consciously or subconsciously. As a child trying to be an adult, from your childish perspective, you appear immature and might feel out of place with your peers. When you're an adult trying to relive your childhood, you again are immature in appearance and often displaced by other adults. The key is to find a healthy balance from childhood to adulthood while maintaining your identity.

When you are a child, you experience life as a child. Everything seems like rules and boundaries that constantly limit you and control you. The truth is, as we learn after getting older, those rules and boundaries are put in place for our own safety, as well as to guide us appropriately into and through adulthood. Getting older as a child doesn't ever seem to happen quickly enough, but if we rush growing up, we will miss important lessons along the way that end up limiting us as adults. Some of us have had childhoods that we are not proud of or that we wish we could hastily erase, while many have enjoyed their childhood thoroughly and look back in admiration. In either case, some people can't escape their childhood as they get older. They can't grow up. As I stated at the beginning of this chapter, getting older is inevitable.

An adult that can't grow up, or hasn't grown up, is in one way or another trying to relive their childhood, or simply continuing to live in it. There are countless reasons for this and, although I am not a psychologist, I would like to interject my opinion on the matter. It is possible that, as a child, they enjoyed their life so much that as they got older and became introduced to the realities of the adult world, it was depressing and sad or overwhelmingly complicated. Since their childhood was so pleasant, they reverted to their childish ways and began to act and do the things they enjoyed as a child.

This isn't really all that bad to do. However, acting this way *in place* of being a mature adult is a problem. It often leads to short-fused patience and childish reactions when something doesn't go their way simply because, as a child, everything was easy. They are living in a world that they are actively denying and creating a safe, fictional reality where the problems they don't want to deal with go away. They come across as extremely immature and can be difficult to deal with on an adult level, and must be interacted with as the child they are portraying until they are able to grow up.

There is a healthy middle ground for these people, and they are truly fun to be around and full of energy. They have been able to harness the joy and imagination of their childhood and display it through an adult mind. Let's face it, some of us still love to pull pranks and make dumb jokes and laugh at farts, and some of us will always love the idea of being a princess and feeling like a priceless jewel. As adults, we have responsibilities and obligations to certain levels of maturity, but we shouldn't let our imaginations and silliness die. Maturity is considering the outcome or consequence of our actions before we act. If you know when it is appropriate to be childish and when it is time to be mature, you have the freedom to be yourself everywhere and anywhere.

On the other end of the spectrum, some have had a childhood that was so negatively impactful that they end up mentally trapped at either the age of that experience, or they grow up much slower out of fear and self-preservation. This truly is sad that children even have experiences like these, but it happens every day. So, what happened?

Some children are neglected or abused mentally, emotionally, physically, and/or sexually. Some children are raised through broken family situations, divorce, or even parental death. And there are some children whose lives have been touched by countless different types of trauma. These life experiences all have different and, at the same time, similar effects on the psychological state and development of children.

Again, I am not a psychologist, but I would like to interject my opinion based on my own life experiences and the many things I have learned along the way from the different books I've read and conversations I have had. When a strong negative experience happens, it so often goes untended. It is often said that, "children are resilient", and that they will be 'just fine' because of that. I believe, to a certain extent, that children are resilient, but ultimately, if they do not receive support and therapy for certain specific situations, they will not understand how to cope with growing up. This might cause somebody to put up walls emotionally, trapping themselves in, and get stuck mentally at the age of trauma. They'll get older, but they don't know how to process their experience, and so they live the same age over and over. As their friends are growing up, they are only getting older. Sometimes we get stuck in the age of trauma, and sometimes the trauma just severely slows our growing up; but it doesn't get resolved until it is truly dealt with.

An adult living with unresolved childhood trauma is still living in a false reality but in a different way than a child who doesn't want their childhood to end. They are likely doing it out of the desire to feel protected and subconsciously waiting for someone to help them through it. There is a lot of confusion associated with someone experiencing life this way. You may think, "I don't feel my age", or "I just don't feel like I fit in". You might still be trying to befriend and associate with people that are the age you became stuck at; or have slowly progressed to. It is ok to be at that point if you can recognize it and you are willing to ask for help to move on. Just don't stay stuck. It is not a fulfilling life to be an adult who cannot 'grow up' because you are still hurt inside so much that you are afraid to live.

You may associate yourself with one of these types, or neither. This is just my opinion and you can take it or leave it. Regardless, I would encourage you to get help if you are able to recognize your growth obstacles. It doesn't mean there's anything wrong with you. In fact, just the ability and willingness to take a deeper look at yourself is helping you to grow further. It is so important to understand the difference between growing up and getting older because you can do one without the other, but I recommend doing them both together. Be willing to take a self-assessment of your childhood, or adulthood, depending on where you're at in life. Understanding where you're at is the key to helping you get where you want to go.

Growing up doesn't have to be painful, although getting older might be. Learn about yourself as much as you can and be willing to make corrections or enhancements. Ask someone you trust to give you an honest opinion about how people perceive you and ask what they view as your strengths and your weaknesses. Be open-minded to review. After all, they're just describing the way you are portraying yourself. Don't be afraid to get a few different perspectives. You can collect this information and compare what people are saying about you to see if they are viewing you the way you would like to be viewed. If not, then maybe it is time to ask for help. We all need to grow up at some point, but we don't have to become boring as a result of it. Keep your youthfulness and your childish imagination. You never know when you might need it.

Chapter 6:

WHEN LIFE GIVES YOU LEMONS

It is a well-known saying, "When life gives you lemons, make lemonade". It sounds simple, doesn't it? When you receive something in life that seems sour, bitter, or distasteful, you turn it into something good, something better. In other words, "When life sucks, don't let it". This is much easier said than done and usually words spoken by somebody NOT currently dealing with something difficult TO somebody who is. There is nothing wrong with this effort to help somebody keep a positive outlook in their life. I mean, some of us just need that little extra encouragement to keep on moving forward. But does it really help, or does it just frustrate? And let's consider lemonade versus lemons. Lemons squeezed into lemonade are still sour and still bitter until you add sugar and water.

So, what is the symbolic water and sugar in this concept, and what does it mean to actually make your situation into lemonade? I'll start with the concept of the sugar. When your life is bitter, it's missing the sweet things, or maybe any sweetness at all. If you have ever consumed juice without any sugar, it is very likely that you either had to spit it out, or you forced yourself to swallow it. I am sure that either way it was not without making a disgusted face and some sort of noise expressing your displeasure. The juice needs the sweetness to overcome the bitterness. It's not as if the bitterness leaves, it's just that the sweetness overpowers the bitterness. You might be experiencing bitterness in your life, or your life might just be bitter in your current state of existence.

You need to find your sugar! What is your sugar? That is something I cannot answer specifically to each individual person, but I can help you get started to determine what your sugar might be. Just like in the food world, there are many sources of both natural and artificial sweeteners. The more natural the source, the healthier it is for you. The same goes for this "life sugar" analogy. When you look at the things in your life that sweeten your thoughts, it may be things like your children, your spouse, your friends, etc.. These are natural sweeteners. Artificial sweeteners can be things like addictions: drugs, alcohol, sex, or binge watching you favorite shows, endlessly scrolling social media, or anything else that you use to artificially pacify your situational bitterness. These are just some examples on either side of the sweeteners. I hope that this serves as a spark to your incredible mind to identify your own source of "life sugar".

Now let's talk about the water. Water is the most abundant, most important, and most necessary life-giving source on Earth. We consume it every day to stay hydrated, which allows our bodies to function properly and helps us to heal. We water plants, or rather, plants receive water nearly every day since most plants are wild and are subject to only what precipitates naturally. But we have complete control over the water we receive. We don't need to wait for it by chance or by any process to happen. It's just there all the time. So what does that look like in this concept? Water is a necessary thing in your life. It is what the bitterness exists in. It is what your sweetener is added to; it is life itself. The bitterness is your situation, it's the process, it's the problem; bitterness is not your life, but it certainly can be *in* your life.

So let's put it all together. Your bitter life circumstance is overcome by the sweet things in your life, and your life itself is really the water that it's all mixed into. You have so many opportunities for bad situations. We all have our bitter experiences, but there is a choice to look at the things that sweeten our life and focus on those things in order to overcome the overwhelming taste of bitterness. This all sounds great, and it appears that we've covered all the angles. But what if life doesn't give you lemons? What if life doesn't give you anything?

Sometimes, you find yourself going through life without any outstanding circumstances. Nothing great happens, nothing terrible happens; you just feel like you're going through the motions everyday, and nothing different seems to happen. At this point, maybe you want lemons, maybe you *need* lemons. You don't want something bad to happen to you, but you want *something* to happen. Some of us are just waiting for life to happen, willing to be at the mercy of the universe. That is truly an incredibly unfulfilling way to live. You can't make lemonade without lemons, so what can you do if life singles you out and doesn't even give you lemons? YOU GO GET THEM! You go find the lemon tree, you climb the tree, and you pick your own lemons! Life isn't always going to hand you something, or anything, whether it's good or bad. Sometimes life is growing lemons somewhere and your job is to find them so you can make your lemonade.

Lemonade can be extremely refreshing, especially ice-cold lemonade, perfectly sweetened, soaking in a big glass full of ice on a hot summer day. You could be hoping for something to change at work or a refreshing change in your relationship. Maybe you have a dream that you want to come true, but you haven't taken any action to make any of it a reality. Those are your lemons. Lemons don't have to be bad, but you need them to make lemonade. You are seeking refreshment in your life, but you don't have lemons. Some of the overcoming we do when we have lemons and turn them into lemonade, can actually be refreshments we might not have otherwise received if those lemons of bitterness weren't a part of our life. So learn to embrace the lemons when they are given to you, because they are the beginning of refreshment. And when you need some refreshment, remember how to climb, and go get your lemons.

Chapter 7:

CHECKING YOUR BAGGAGE

At some point, most of us have been on an airplane trip and even a majority of those who have not understand checking your baggage. If you haven't been on an airplane yourself, maybe you've watched in a movie someone checking their baggage. When you are preparing for a trip, there are some common things you do to prepare. There are details that you typically know before heading out as well. Things like where you're going, how long you will be gone, what you will be doing, what the weather will be like, etc.. This helps you to plan and be prepared. You're bringing things with you that you already have, from the place you already are, to a place you're going to be. If you have a lot of things, you will need a larger bag. If you have enough things or if you have certain restricted items that you cannot carry on the plane with you, you will need to check them in a separate bag that you will drop off upon check-in.

In some cases, you may have multiple bags that you need to check. This could be from bringing items for other people, longer trips, or from picking up extra things during a trip you are returning from. When you get to the airport, you leave your baggage and are no longer burdened with trying to carry it through the airport during your travel. You can make your way around feeling relieved, knowing that your baggage is going to be taken care of. In my experience, once the bags are checked nobody speaks about them or their contents for the remainder of the journey until you have reached your destination. If we use this analogy to understand our relationships, it could help teach us how to move on and have healthy relationships.

As we live our lives we collect things: material things, ideas, emotions, memories, experiences, and so on. These are all items that we carry with us throughout our lives and sometimes never let go; but much like the things in our lives that we might pack in a suitcase, these personal things age with time and get worn out, or simply become outdated and need to be removed from our lives or replaced with something newer. Some people hang onto everything they have ever come across or received. We know them as "hoarders". They cannot let go of things and, therefore, try to live in the past and present at the same time, making limited room for the future.

When you hold onto every single moment in your life, both good and bad, you become an emotional hoarder. When your emotions and experiences are strongly negative or traumatic and you continue to carry all of that with you, you end up living in the past, struggling in the present, and leaving limited room for your future. Your future emotions, your future experiences, your future relationships, your future happiness.

When you have traumatic experiences in your life, those memories and thought processes that arose out of that situation, or situations, are dangerous items to take into a new relationship. Those are things that would be necessary to "check" when you are getting ready to board the plane for your next trip. Carrying dangerous things in the airport and trying to get them through security could get you into quite a bit of trouble. There are people in place as you go through the security protocol whose job it is to ensure the safety of all people around you both now and on your journey to your destination.

When you attempt to bring prohibited items with you, whether knowingly or otherwise, those prohibited items are taken from you without compromise. They are not concerned with whether or not you need or want the items, and they are not concerned with whether or not you are prepared to give them up. You don't want to take on a new relationship with prohibited items from your past because they may be taken from you before you are prepared to let them go. When you lose something, or something is taken from you, it is a much different feeling than giving it away when you're ready.

If you are not in control of when and how your experiences or emotions are removed from your life, it causes further problems and is more emotionally damaging. When you start a new relationship, that person doesn't know what you've been through and sometimes they don't, or can't, understand. They just want to get rid of things for you. Some stuff you might not be ready to let go of, but *why* you're not ready to let go of it is very important. You don't want to bring "baggage" into a new part of your life because that usually equates to drama, and nobody really volunteers for extra drama. Sometimes your friends care so much about you that they want to get rid of things for you and press you to move on from past experiences. It is much easier said than done.

These people are in a position to refuse to allow prohibited items you are still carrying with you, from going with you into your future. They are your security screening process. But they aren't necessarily concerned with whether or not you're ready to let it go. It is not safe for your future relationships to carry these things forward, and it is important to check this baggage when you are going somewhere new in your life. If you learn to check your baggage, you can let it go and you no longer have to worry about the burden it is to carry with you.

Someone else takes it for you with the assurance that they will take care of it from here on out. Your baggage can be checked with a therapist, a close friend, trusted family, or another respected person. You can only check your baggage if it is packed up. This means that you will need to deal with it and sort through it in a way that is healthy and safe, and in a way that you feel good letting it go. When you check your bag at the airport, you don't get to go back to it. You actually have zero access to your baggage and cannot get to it even if you wanted. You have entrusted your baggage with someone else and you know everything is going to be ok. Your hands are free to handle your carry-on items as you travel to your new destination.

There are acceptable items from your past that you can take with you, but they are limited in quantity and are things you need or use often. These are positive thoughts and memories, along with skills and personality traits you have developed over time through previous relationships or experiences. They are good to take with you on your new adventure. In most cases, they make the travel through your new relationship more pleasant.

What things do you take with you into new relationships that are positive and healthy? Take a few minutes to do a self-inventory of the carry-on items you currently hold and the things you would like to have with you. This may require you to get a second opinion from a trusted source. After all, sometimes you don't think of something you would like to take with you on the plane until you see someone else with it, and then you prepare it for your next journey. Once you've done this, you can compare what you have with what you want. This can help you to come up with a plan to create healthier relationships or, in other words, a more pleasant journey.

I started saving up my life events at a very young age. I didn't really know what I was doing but it was still happening. The more baggage I acquired, the more exhausted and burdened I became. Since I didn't deal with any security protocols along the way and didn't have many relationships, I never had to check any baggage. When I mention relationships, I am referring to all relationships not just intimate personal relationships like a serious partner or spouse. I am talking about friends, siblings, parents, extended family, colleagues, and any other types of relationships you may develop. All relationships are important and each in their own way. If you try to bring your baggage into these relationships where they don't belong you will have things taken from you, and it will only cause you deeper wounds. I learned all of this the hard way.

When I would develop a new relationship or try to grow with an existing one, I would eventually hit a wall. I would develop a relationship to a certain point and it would always stall out, or I would become insecure and feel the thoughts of rejection flooding in and I would open my suitcase to use the things I had. The problem was that the suitcase was my baggage, full of the things I didn't really need. A lot of which were actually prohibited items. They were the things I had experienced in the past and the memories, thoughts, and unresolved traumas that were damaging me and my efforts to grow.

I didn't know that I was supposed to get rid of these things or that they were even dangerous to my new relationships. I just knew that it was all familiar to me and so, in a way, I was comforted by familiarity. But comfort and familiarity were not helping me to move forward in my relationships, it was holding me back. The most important relationship that I needed was struggling the most; my relationship with myself.

I had not learned how to have a relationship with myself, and because of that I could not fully understand how to have a relationship with anybody else. I didn't know how to love myself or that loving myself was even a thing. I had no idea how crucial it was to start loving me. If you can't love yourself, how can you expect to truly love anybody else? All your relationships are going to be a direct reflection of how you love yourself. If you are insecure about yourself, whether in general or in specific details, you will find yourself having those same insecurities in other people as you try to develop relationships with them.

If you have a lot of self-shame, you feel as if other people see you with shame, and it causes you to act in a way that you feel protects you from those people. You might distance yourself or only talk about certain things, and you might have an overwhelming sense of never feeling like you will be good enough or that people are constantly judging you because of whatever you're ashamed of. Those people that are strangers to you, and even some that are not, have no idea what shame you might have! Only if you tell them. But why would you? You don't have to feel ashamed of yourself for anything. If you feel this way, then be strong enough to seek a professional solution, but don't take it with you. Relieve yourself of your self-laid burdens and check your baggage. It is ok to let go of the things of the past and make room for the things of your future.

I try not to look back at my traumas and experiences and wish that something would have happened differently. The fact of the matter is, these things have already happened and can't be undone, unexperienced, or "un-happen". What I have spent a lot of time and energy doing is learning how to understand these things and what to learn from them. I do my best to get my baggage sorted out so I know what I need to get rid of before it goes through the x-ray, and everything I shouldn't have is exposed and taken from me. I want to know ahead of time so I have the opportunity to properly remove what I don't need. I want to be able to check that baggage and forget about it, knowing that someone else will take care of it from here. I don't want to be burdened with bad memories, lies, hurts, pains, and traumas from the past. I want to build healthy relationships without putting other people in danger.

When you take the time to reflect on yourself to learn about your baggage and sort through the good and the bad, you give yourself room to grow. It has been said that, "knowledge is power". That means that self-knowledge is self-empowerment. If the more you know about yourself and the more and better you love yourself, the better all your other relationships will be; then it should be your goal to get to know yourself as intimately as possible. If you feel like you're hitting a wall or you are having the same struggles in all your relationships, maybe it is time to step back and take a look at how you are relating to yourself. Make sure you're checking your baggage *before* you go on your next trip, it will be more fun for everyone.

Chapter 8:

HEART MURMURS

Since I was a teenager I have had doctors tell me they could hear a heart murmur when they listened to my heart. In most cases, I was told it was nothing to be concerned about and they were not worried. But it is an abnormality with one of the most crucial systems in my body, *I* was concerned. Why was it happening, and why was it not concerning? I really like to be in the know and understand what is happening to my body. I want to enjoy life without having a constant fear that something bad could happen or is about to happen.

It has been studied that between 40%-45% of children are diagnosed with having a heart murmur, decreasing to approximately 10% in adulthood. There are varying degrees of severity regarding heart murmurs that are used to determine the risk of each individual. I have been fortunate enough to be on the low end of the scale and have only intermittently been diagnosed with a murmur. I have experienced significant heart-related situations over the years that have been investigated by cardiologists and electrophysiologists, from which I am able to draw some of these insights and conclusions.

A heart murmur is a sound that occurs between heartbeats, that is abnormal, and usually does not have a major effect. There are times that it can be related to an underlying heart condition, which can be what leads to concern. Our hearts are very complex and use electrical impulses and physical contractions with moving parts to pump blood throughout our entire body. When we have good blood flow, our other systems are able to function properly and can even bring healing to the different parts of our body.

Our blood is our life, we simply cannot live without it and need it to flow properly 24 hours a day in order to keep living. When we have a heart murmur, it can affect the flow of life moving throughout our bodies and limit the capacities of our life-giving systems. We don't have major concerns over small changes, but over time those small changes can add up to big problems. We slowly die as the flow becomes limited and, the more interrupted our flow, the quicker our bodies will begin to change and begin to shut down.

If I were to give the effect of heart murmurs a place in understanding life's relationships, I would say it is a way to understand love itself. Love is the life flow of all relationships. Without it, your relationships die; sometimes slowly, and sometimes much quicker. This is an obvious argument since the heart is so easily and so often the symbol of love. The abnormality in love, or the experience of it, would be your murmur. We all experience love in different ways, and not all of us will experience the murmurs of love. Some people are able to go through life with great examples and experiences of love without having to feel abnormalities. Those that do have varying degrees of severity.

Somebody who has experienced a small love hurt, or a low degree of murmur, would maybe have had somebody they know loves them break a promise or disappoint them. I think most, if not all, of us have heard this murmur. It is a very common occurrence to be let down, disappointed, or have someone break a simple promise. It hurts. It might be small and not incredibly significant overall but, at the time, it is concerning. When this happened to me I thought it was a big deal, that it was not normal and that it should be corrected. I didn't want to live my life worrying that somebody might do this again, even though it was extremely common and very likely to happen again with little residual effect.

The truth is, it affects the life flow and love flow of every relationship in the future, whether you notice it or not. It might not affect you on a day to day basis, but it is slowly going after the fullness of love in all current and future relationships. I didn't struggle so much that I couldn't build healthy new relationships or continue to develop the current ones, but there was almost a small voice in my head, or my heart, that quietly warned of the possibility of being hurt again. This birthed the feeling of skepticism in relationships. I subconsciously began to question relationships and the intent of those involved. I started to subconciously question everything.

The next degree of severity I'll just refer to as a "middle" level murmur. This is when a low-degree murmur has gone too long unchecked or untreated and has worsened. The ones you love are lying to you repeatedly. They may be taking advantage of you, avoiding you out of passivity, or intentionally excluding you. This kind of murmur hurts. This is when the love flow becomes noticeably restricted or interrupted. You're getting to the point in your life where you know you've got a problem but you think you are unable to do anything about it, so you end up living with it. It still kills your relationships slowly, but it has increased its pace. When I experienced this, I started to withdraw from the people who were causing this blockage, but not completely.

I allowed them to continue in my life without resolve. I didn't do anything to protect myself. I didn't take any corrective action. I just let this restriction of flow tear apart my relationships one by one. I couldn't let anybody get close anymore. It was as if I had put up a glass wall all around me so I could see out and they could see in, but we would no longer be in real contact. I didn't feel safe any longer to let anyone get too close to me. There was still a glass door in my wall; this allowed for the *possibility* of a relationship, eventually. I felt myself harboring unnecessary bitterness, and sometimes that bitterness was delivered to an undeserving party.

My "love flow" was restricted. I was not able to fully love anymore, and I was not doing anything to get better. I simply accepted my situation in life as the new normal. I didn't know that I was actually dying in the sense of my relationships and my ability to love freely. I was not able to grow in the relationships I currently had, and I struggled even more to start new ones. If I did, I would be very skeptical of those new people I was allowing in my life because I didn't know their intentions, and I was so injured that I couldn't believe they just wanted to be a friend, a brother, a spouse.

The worst and most serious degree of murmur is just that, dangerous. This is the type of murmur that is usually caused by an underlying condition and can require surgery to correct it. It is very noticeable and very consistent. I would compare this to being devastated or traumatized in a very close and very intimate relationship. As I say 'intimate', I am not just talking about sexual intimacy, but anyone you become so comfortably close with you allow them to see inside your life, to know what is in your head and in your heart.

After all, let's just consider the best way to describe intimacy being 'into me, you see'. This is someone like a very close sibling, parent, or other family member, or a very close best friend or spouse. These are people that you don't ever expect to intentionally hurt you or cause you harm. These people have very special access to your love flow. They can cause some severe interruptions, as the underlying condition, and bring you further long-term damage to all relationships, both present and future.

Your murmur is the lasting pain caused by the event, or events, of these individuals' negative actions. I have only experienced this a small number of times in my life, but I can assure you, without "surgery", this will not go away. You will need to get help, and you will need to take care of correcting this problem. I found myself having to get away from those people altogether and get rid of the evidence and memories that I had constantly in front of me. That was just the beginning. I then spent countless hours over months just sorting through the causes of my murmurs.

Since I had allowed them to not only accumulate in number over the years but also in severity by not ever taking care of myself from past situations, I had compounded the effects dramatically. I was to the point that my love flow would become intermittently blocked or flow wide open without regulation. I was either loving full-on like a firehose, or I had nothing to give and would begin destroying relationships, sometimes before they ever started.

I was completely untrusting to every single person in my life and every new person I met. I went out of my way to intentionally avoid people just so I wouldn't have to talk to them and pretend to care. There were so many times I just felt so worthless and incapable because I believed I was the broken one and there was something wrong with me. I believed that I had messed everything up and that I would never get it right. I thought everybody wanted to hurt me, everybody wanted to use me, everybody wanted something from me.

I had no desire to help anyone, no desire to get to know anybody, and became extremely irritated when I was forced into a position to "make friends". I wanted nothing to do with people, with *any* people. Even the ones I considered my closest and most intimate relationships, I could no longer allow in. It no longer mattered if I had walls, doors, gates, or whatever. I had secluded myself in a relational bunker and buried it a mile underground. I wasn't leaving, and nobody was coming in. I was safe when I was alone, and that's all I was concerned about.

My love flow was severely damaged, I was emotionally dying. I felt as though I no longer had the capacity for love, neither to give nor receive. This was the problem though; I had the ability for love and relationships, but I was dying because the lifeblood of my relationships was being cut off. I had so many terrible thoughts during that process of diagnosis and healing. I wanted to hurt myself, and I wanted to hurt other people, even people I didn't know and had never met. I was reckless. The problem wasn't with everyone else; they were just the cause. The problem was that I never got the necessary healing to recover and just allowed myself to be run down, and I accepted defeat. The reason we have doctors and modern medicine is so that things that cause us great pain can be dealt with and healed through a process involving other people who have learned about what we are dealing with and know how to help.

Your "doctors" for these ailments are likely going to be, at the most extreme point, psychologists and therapists. Friends and family can, and usually do, help you along the way to get through the small stuff.

At some point though, things may get so bad that you need to seek help from a professional who is trained and experienced to help you in the way that you truly need. It is ok to get surgery and be healed of physical deformities and abnormalities, and to repair physical brokenness. Likewise, it is ok to get the same kind of help to heal from emotional and relational ailments.

Chapter 9:

TRENCHING PEBBLES

This is exactly what it sounds like. Have you ever tried to dig a trench through a pile of pebbles, or maybe in the sand at the beach? It is an extremely frustrating, physically demanding process. I wouldn't expect the majority of people to have been through this exact scenario, but I do believe most people can relate to the struggle. I have personally struggled through this process and coincidentally, I was struggling through the real-life metaphorical process simultaneously.

There was a project I was working on once that required the use of a large pile of pebbles, maybe 30-40 tons. I had laid them out and realized that I should have put in some piping that I was going to be burying before laying out the pebbles. It is incredible how hindsight can be so obvious about the decisions you should have made or made differently. Often times, we set up our own struggles simply by making poor choices to begin with. If our foresight was as obviously transparent as our hindsight, life would be different for all of us. I still had to bury the piping, and life still goes on.

I worked in the heat of the day to begin digging these trenches, adding stress to stress. I already had the frustration of not doing this in a sensible order but undoing the pebbles was not an option, so I began to trench my way through the ocean of tiny rocks that seemed to work against me with every effort of my shovel. Every time I would dig out a shovel-full, the sides would slide back in. Again, and again, and again. My effort was getting me nowhere but exhausted and more frustrated. It didn't matter that I wanted the trench, it didn't matter that I wanted the walls of the trench to stay in place, it didn't matter that I was giving my full effort.

This trench was going to take incredible commitment. It might seem like an impossible situation you've gotten yourself into, where every effort is seemingly undone, and at times, it feels like your efforts are working against you. You can't undo some things that you have done, and you can't change some situations once you're in them. You *can* decide to keep going, though, and see it through to the end.

With the hot sun focused on melting my head, and as the walls continued to cave in, I would wipe the sweat running down my face, look back at my progress, and then look forward at how much was left to do. It quickly became overwhelming to look at where I had to go and how much work it was going to take to get there, regardless of the progress I had already made. It felt never-ending as if it wouldn't matter how hard I tried or how bad I wanted it, accomplishing it just wasn't going to happen. It was as if as soon as I looked forward, I had forgotten every single ounce of progress I had made and what I had accomplished.

Even as I got the trench to stay open, the weight of the rocks I was digging out and placing to the side was shifting and causing the walls to collapse behind me. As I walked around the trench, as carefully and mindful as I could, I still caused some shifting and collapsing of the trench I had completed. By my own effort of trying to move forward, and trying to resolve doing the right things, I felt as though I was working against myself and creating more work in the repetition of constantly digging the same hole over and over. It was a vain attempt, so I thought, to repeat my efforts in my situation to achieve results. I so quickly forgot that I really *was* making progress. It was just slower than I wanted.

We don't always see our progress when it is slow, but even slow progress is progress. My effort wasn't in vain to be so redundant. It wasn't about the speed of completion. It was about completion. It was about committing to the process and knowing that as long as I didn't quit, I would make it to the end. It is ok to be exhausted, it's ok to stop for water, it is ok to ask for help.

After taking a few minutes to rehydrate and encourage myself to continue to the end, I went back to work in the trenches. I had to finish this project; it needed to be done, and nobody else was going to do it for me. You are going to have things that are necessary to do, things you will need to do for yourself, things that need to be done by you and nobody else. It isn't always going to be easy. Maybe it will never be easy, but you still have to do it. My body was aching all over, my back was sore, my arms hurt, and I was frustrated and exhausted. I had been digging through these trenches for over 4 hours. I felt hopeless in my efforts because the closer I got to the end, the more difficult it was to keep going. I had to keep reminding myself that it was almost over, that it wasn't going to last forever.

I managed to fight through the cramps and the aches and pains, the external factors like the heat from the sun and the dry, unbreathable, dust-filled air, and I finished the trenches. I was so relieved. The effort I put in was finally validated by the visual result of the trenches. Now everyone could see what I had done, but they didn't know how much it took from me to get there. I laid down my piping and, as was the purpose of the trenches in the first place, I buried it. I covered up the intense, sacrificing, exhausting work I had just been so proud and satisfied to have completed. Only to bury my progress in purpose.

Now I have all this piping in the rocks, the trenches that were once there, filled in. It was as if I had never been there in the first place. Like all that work didn't ever happen, it didn't exist. Not a single person could see, nor would they ever know what I did, unless I told them. All the efforts I made for myself were buried, but I remembered. I gave all my effort to accomplish something that needed to be done. I did it for me.

There was a purpose for all this effort. The work I put into this part of the project laid the unseen groundwork for something more. There was a bigger purpose to my exhausting commitment. I was now stronger; I was satisfied with myself for completing the task I set out to do. Sometimes, we end up going through a process of suffering and sacrifice so someone else doesn't have to. So commonly, parents will do this for their children, spouses will do this for their partner, and friends will do this for their closest friends. They sacrifice their own comfort. They work out the details that nobody else sees, and nobody else will ever know about because either they're the only one qualified to do it or they're the only one truly willing to do it. The sacrifice you make, whether it is for yourself or someone you love, it matters. You do it so the ones you love don't have to.

There's an appropriate sense of pride and satisfaction that comes from accomplishment through tremendous struggle. When you love somebody, or even if the trenches are for yourself, you'll do anything to take away unnecessary struggle. Don't give up before you finish your process because if it wasn't important, you wouldn't be doing it in the first place. Whatever you're trenching pebbles through, it is worth the effort, it is worth struggling, it is worth fighting through. You will have something that you're proud of, and when you're proud of yourself, you're unstoppable.

Chapter 10:

WHEN HOPE IS LOST

When I was a child, I hoped *for* things. As I grew up, I understood more about life and I began to hope *in* things. I suppose a part of that change in thought process was because I had come to a place in my life where I was more concerned for things to happen than to appear. I was not as concerned about getting all my Christmas gifts, birthday presents, or whatever gifting holiday may relate to you because the things in my life were no longer as important as the experiences in my life. I stopped hoping for birthday presents and started hoping to have a birthday. Instead of being hopeful for Christmas presents, I was hopeful just to be able to spend it with my family. In fact, every holiday became an event of hope, cherishing the opportunity to share some quality time with the ones that matter most. I am hopeful for the outcome of events. I hope in health situations, like surgery or severe illness. I hope in legal battles for favorable outcomes, I hope in relationships to stay healthy, I hope in my financial stability, I hope in my friends and family to prosper, and I hope in the successes of my children. Having hope is such a great feeling, life-giving in a way. I feel weightless and in control of myself when I have hope. I feel so confident in myself and my life circumstances. I feel almost invincible, ready to take on whatever the world has to throw at me.

When there is hope, there is peace. When hope is lost, there is chaos. In my opinion, there is nothing more powerfully destructive in this world than hopelessness. I really believe there is nothing that eats away at a person more dramatically than feeling hopeless. This is how people get to the 'end of their rope', their 'last thread', where they just completely give up. They feel no hope, no reason to continue, no positive possible outcome, and the absence of peace.

Hopelessness is to be held captive by fear. The peace that you once had in hope has now been replaced by the darkness of fear in hopelessness. You give away all control to your own fears that nothing is going to end well for you, that there is no point in trying any longer, and that hoping for the good is pointless and unimaginably impossible. Hopelessness is destructive and almost inevitably leads to depression. In fact, if I had to define depression, I would use the word "hopeless" and maybe only that word.

When I consider the many times I felt depressed, I would be able to point out the specific hopelessness in certain areas of my life. I just wanted to give up because I saw absolutely zero possibility of succeeding. So I thought, "What's the point?". The thought of giving any effort whatsoever to something whose outcome would be not at all favorable to me, or so I believed, was overwhelming, exhausting, and even a bit irritating.

I have been through some very dark times of hopelessness. At best, I would say I crawled through those times because of how worn out I was, but that would be an understatement. There were times when I didn't even have the energy or desire to crawl. The best I could do was take the chance that somebody might trip over me, lying in the middle of the road and send me rolling downhill into some sort of action. I had this desire to just be disposed of, but not by my own doing. I was too exhausted to even try to hurt myself, but I also wasn't taking care of myself because I just stopped caring. I stopped believing in a resolution. I stopped hoping. I have been to the edge, and I have set up camp there and stayed for weeks on end. I had no problem staying lost in hopelessness, lost in fear and chaos, living completely in darkness.

I try to justify it looking back as if I was protecting myself, but it wasn't protection from the right things. I was protecting myself from the solution, but out of fear I was convincing myself I was protecting myself from being hurt. I was already hopeless, so I didn't think anything more or worse could come from secluding myself. I forced myself to live in constant fear, and fear became familiar, and familiar became fearful. I became fearful of hope; I didn't want to let anybody in, especially those who wanted to help. I didn't know how. I was hopeless, and they just didn't understand what I was going through. I couldn't make them understand, and I didn't care to try. That was too much effort.

I lost all hope going through a few different situations in my life. The worst experience I think I can recall was a time when I was fighting a divorce and custody battle. I know that not everybody will relate to this but unfortunately, a lot of people will. I had hoped for results in each case hearing time and time again but, consistently, I was let down. My hope was crushed, stolen from me in a way that was eventually irreparable, at least not in my own efforts. I had placed my hope in others, people I trusted, people I loved and cared about, people that had once given me hope. It is so damaging to have hope stolen and crushed that hopelessness is easier than trying to hope again. I developed an intense fear of hope.

I was traumatized by hope. I couldn't handle hoping for anything. Birthdays, holidays, special events, and any other situations that put me in a position to hope in people were terrifying. My health, my finances, and my relationships I had hopelessly given up on. I had such a lack of hope for improvement in any of these circumstances that I stopped trying, and I stopped connecting. I would, occasionally, get empowered by something somebody said or did or feel a glimmer of hope in a situation, only to be crushed again and again.

When I lost all hope, I began to tell myself that to hope was foolish, that 'to hope' was dangerous. I settled into hopelessness as a way of life. It became routine to look only at the negative side of every single thing in my life, as well as everyone else's lives. I couldn't even have hope for someone else when they had hope for themselves. There may have even been times that I was responsible for stealing hope away from somebody when they just wanted support. I am not proud of that, nor am I going to begin to justify my actions, but if I had lost all hope, I couldn't encourage someone else that hope was even logical or real. There was a part of me that was afraid to be hopeful because if my hope was fulfilled, then I would be proved wrong in my hopelessness. I would have negated my reasons for behaving the way I did. So truthfully, there was a significant amount of pride that kept me hopeless, fearful, and stubborn to receive help or to pursue or believe in hope.

With hopelessness, depression, and fear, I developed an overwhelming anxiety in my everyday life. It was difficult for me to do anything, go anywhere, or try to commit to anything. I was unreliable and full of excuses. I never wanted to go anywhere, even when I had to or was expected to. I made my home my safe place. When I was home, I was protected from everything outside of those four walls. I could hide and disappear; I was able to safely disconnect from the world. If somebody called me, I just didn't answer. I rarely responded to messages and voicemails, if I even checked them at all.

There were days that I wouldn't get dressed, I would hardly eat, and there were days I didn't talk to a single person or even leave the house. I wouldn't even go outside to check the mail. There was nothing that was going to convince me to leave my safe place. People wanted to come visit me because of my sheltered condition, but when anybody came to my safe place, I felt invaded. I felt as if they were coming into "my space" and intruding where I felt protected. When somebody visited, I felt threatened because my personal space was no longer my own. I would push through the intense anxiety of the company of others until they were gone and I got my space back.

Often times, people would invite or request that I attend events or just get out of the house and visit with them. I had no interest in leaving my home and certainly did not want to commit to any kind of obligation. There were times that I reluctantly forced myself up and out of my house. These times were filled with all kinds of negative and begrudging emotions. I was already depressed and hopeless, I didn't need or want to go out and be around people that were happy and hopeful. They always wanted to cheer me up when I was visibly distraught, but that's not what I wanted. I wanted to be miserable and sulk. I wanted to be hopeless because, in my mind, there was no hope and no reason to be hopeful. I felt broken like I had completely failed at life and there were no more second chances.

There was nothing I could do, or at that point wanted to do, to change my situation. I remember every time I would go out, regardless of who I was with or what I was doing, I had the same thought process. I was somewhat content to be out of the house and around real people but all I could think, all my mind could focus on, was this one thought, "I just want to go home". All I could do was squirm in my skin and think about every possible reason and excuse to leave wherever and whatever I was doing and go home. It wasn't anything wrong with the people or the activity, I just didn't want to be out. I wanted to be home; home was safe. I was so depressed that I almost couldn't function. I couldn't think right. I wasn't hungry; nothing brought me joy; nothing was fun or funny, and the best people in my life could, at best, bring me to light for a matter of seconds. I was buried and drowning in hopelessness with no end in sight.

It took many weeks, quite honestly I think it was months, to overcome this terrible depression and anxiety brought on by my own hopelessness. I tried, not very hard, to get over it on my own and, to no surprise, failed miserably. It was like someone sinking in quicksand, trying to pull themselves out by pulling one hand with the other. If you're sinking, you need someone else to pull you out, but you must let go of yourself in order to grab onto something, or someone, that can help save you. And beyond that, you need to hang on!

You can't just hold on until it gets difficult and then let go believing the other person failed you. You are the one who let go; they are still pulling and reaching for you, but you gave up on yourself. There will always be at least one person in your life who is willing to fight for you. It might not always be the same person, but somebody will always be there, even if they tag team like a relay race. If hope can be lost, then hope can be found. Sometimes, you just need help to find it. Sometimes, you need somebody to help you see things that are right in front of you. Sometimes, you're so focused on pulling yourself out that you don't look up at the rope that is being offered to you that will pull you to safety. Look up, reach out, and once again take hold of your hope.

Chapter 11:

PULLING OUT THE DAGGER

I have been a very trusting person my whole life. There were times I should have been more cautious, but the hindsight of all those situations were obviously much clearer than the previously present moments. When I first meet somebody I have this gut feeling combined with situational awareness that I typically use to determine the level of trust I want to place in any particular person. The same goes for any new or unfamiliar environmental situations; I am hyper-observant to my surroundings when they are new or unfamiliar. I wasn't always so careful. This state of meta-awareness has been developed over years of trauma and disappointment. I can say for myself as I was growing up I would place my trust in new people, and situations in new environments, in the guardians of my surroundings. My parents would bring me places and introduce me to people they would, I believe, trust to not harm me.

My Boy Scout and church leaders would be trained in situational awareness and youth protection, so again, I believed they would only introduce me to people and places that would not endanger my wellbeing. Through their judgement, and their actions, I built my own standard of trust, judgement, and morals. However, when I was a teenager, the people I allowed to place influence in the decision-making aspect of my life included my peers. Not all of them had been brought up in an appropriate environment, or they simply lacked the experience in judgement. This created a challenge for me mentally and emotionally. I wanted to fit in, like every kid, but at the same time I wanted to preserve my integrity and safety. I tried to lapse judgement to participate in situations that weren't dangerous but also were not the best thing to do. I did things that were unsafe because, well, everyone else I was with at the time was doing it. This process of personal development and fitting in is what we likely all go through to some degree as we grow up.

When you meet somebody new, you want to give them the benefit of the doubt that their intent is not to cause you great harm. You give them a kind of open-door opportunity to do good while hoping they don't do you wrong. After you know someone for a little while, depending on the time you've spent with them, you begin to truly trust them because you have developed a relationship. You begin to think they are not going to hurt you. You are born into and with your family and your extended family. There is usually a free pass for them to operate in your life without worrying if they will cause you harm.

Let's face it, kids are going to have some sort of arguments growing up together and might hurt each other incidentally, but nothing major usually happens under normal circumstances. You might grow up trusting your family to protect you and look out for you but, the truth is, you don't know what you don't know. When you are a child, you don't understand right and wrong until it is taught to you, you don't understand danger until you get hurt, and you don't know that somebody is going to harm you until after it happens. The family surrounding you is thought to be your safe place, and with it the protection from painful situations and poor decision-making.

Many people don't get to experience a trouble-free, pain-free upbringing. So many people that I know personally have been through some relationally troubled past. They have experienced family allowing dangerous environments or people in their lives, friends betraying them, broken promises, misleading statements, major disappointments, discounted beliefs or emotions, and so on. Each one of those experiences creates a memory. A memory that is branded into the emotional and psychological processes that dictate your ability to trust and judge your situations.

It slowly, piece by piece, rearranges your thoughts to become subconsciously protective of yourself in every situation, regardless of your surroundings. You begin to trust less on the front end and become skeptical of anyone and everyone. It starts out simple and unnoticeable to yourself. Maybe you still meet or get introduced to somebody new, shake hands, smile, and give a friendly greeting, but there is a quiet part of you controlling the once-present freedom to invite them into your life with an open door. Perhaps you would have immediately gone into a detailed story about your life with anybody you met, giving full trust to someone new because, in your naivety of experience, you had no reason to hold back.

Your quiet internal process stops you from giving any real details until you eventually just give a quiet smile, possibly a greeting, and remain externally silent while your mind is racing uncontrollably, thinking of any and all ways this person could hurt you. The same goes for environmental trust. You may have once completely been unguarded in every environment but as you experience more and more of life, you start to post mental guards in every room, every situation.

Before, you didn't have a guard to put down. Now, you have to practically blackmail your own mental guard to stand down. You may walk into a room and immediately take an assessment of every person in the room, check out every angle, look at every door, every window, every table and chair, the lights, the cameras, etc., and determine if you are safe there if you can remain safe there; and if your safety is jeopardized, you already have an escape plan.

This is the result of years of bad experiences, not just an overnight change. It's not unlikely that somebody had one incredibly terrifying experience that brought them to this point, but typically, this process takes time over multiple experiences. The most painful part of this process is that you were more than likely harmed in some way by someone you trusted or by something that was once familiar and safe. When we build trust in a situation or in specific people, we simultaneously develop an understanding that we are safe because we have that trust. When you meet a significant other and develop a close, intimate relationship, you might even get married - You trust them.

he more time you spend with somebody the more open you are with them, and the more you think they will never hurt you because they love you. You might think, "Why would they hurt me?". When you have your own home, you begin to feel comfortable and safe there, but the second somebody violates your safe space and breaks your trust in your environment you might put in an alarmed security system complete with cameras and recording devices, or perhaps even a safe room. This is all for your own protection and, possibly at some point, for the protection of others.

As we develop closer, more intimate relationships or become deeply familiar with our surroundings, we tend to let our guard down because we start to believe those people and places will never hurt us, as if the capacity for pain and danger were non-existent. I am not saying to be so careful that you never get comfortable, and always end up on guard no matter what happens or who somebody is. That would go completely against what I am trying to do here. What I am saying is; this happens, and when it happens, it is important to know what to do about it.

Before you can know how to pull out the dagger, you should first understand how the dagger got there in the first place. When swords were a more common form of battle, a person would have to face their attacker head-on, face to face, hand to hand. You looked into each other's eyes as you slashed and stabbed at each other, hoping for mortal dominance. They were trying to kill you, and you were trying to kill them, but neither wanted to die. Self-preservation, and very likely honor, were your driving forces to stay alive. There was something you believed in, that you were unwavering in, that you were willing to die to uphold. Your morals and standards are no different.

Like the soldiers and warriors of old battles, you were brought up under a certain belief system and experienced life through that system, creating your judgements, your beliefs, your ability and your willingness to trust. If you were battling with a sword, normally you did not personally know or have a relationship with that person. You were simply enemies on opposing sides of beliefs. Sometimes you would know the person quite well and it truly was a difference of opinion, a significant difference, that caused you to go toe to toe with swords. You might have trusted this person at one point, and because of some external factor, they no longer believed the same as you, and it was conflicting enough to cause a fight. On the other hand, they might have been close to you and done something to violate you or your space, such as an affair or a delicate broken promise, and you were hurt and angered to the point of aggression. But that's a sword; what about a dagger?

To effectively use a dagger, you must be close enough to use it. A dagger can be used in surprise, such as a person coming out of the crowd and lunging to stab at you. But more often than not, a dagger is used by someone who has close, intimate access to you and your life. A close family member, a well-trusted friend, a spouse, even a child. They need to be close enough to you that they're within arm's reach, close enough that you wouldn't expect it. There are two ways to get stabbed with a dagger: in the front and in the back.

When you are stabbed in the front, it is usually from somebody very, very close in relationship to you. Someone who can be close enough to share your personal space. They have already planned to hurt you for some time beforehand and are prepared to hurt you by bringing the dagger. There is a fair amount of deceit involved with this maneuver because they are so close to you and act as if they still care for you and still have concern for you. You don't see it coming, but they are patiently waiting to strike at just the right moment when you least expect it. They are planning to hurt you when you are defenseless. There is no chance for you to know this is going to happen because they're not going to tell you even if you asked, even if somehow you could have discovered they were up to something. It is motivated by something deeply personal.

Maybe you unintentionally hurt them or let them down, or maybe it was intentional and you wanted to hurt them, but you didn't expect this kind of recourse. When you get a dagger in the front, you are face-to-face with your aggressor, they're looking you right in the eyes when they hurt you. Waves of emotion and swirling thoughts flood your mind, but floating their way to the surface through all that pain is the buoy of betrayal. Betrayal floats above every other thought; it doesn't sink, and you don't forget it. It sits on top of every future experience in every relationship from that point forward, causing you to always expect the same results when you find yourself in familiar situations. You remember the pain of the dagger and the look in their eyes, and you can't help but crumble inside.

When you are stabbed in the back, you certainly don't see it coming, but the situation is different. You're either leaving a situation, whether running or walking, or they sneak up on you. It is something that an enemy would do when you are retreating or trying to escape. If you're running away, you're trying to return to a safe place. But sometimes it's not the enemy, sometimes it is the person that again is close to you. You trust them enough that you would even turn your back toward them because rather than plunge a dagger into it, you trust them to watch and protect your back. They are angry, possibly jealous, and they still have some sort of respect for you or fear of you. They are not comfortable facing you about their unsettled feelings but rather they want to take advantage of an opportunity to take you down when you are most vulnerable. They want you to look bad, they don't want you to succeed, they might be afraid that you'll find out who did it, so they stab you in the back quickly and then turn to run away while you're piled face first on the floor. This is an especially painful hurt because sometimes, you really don't know who hurt you, and you might never know. You begin to live in constant fear and are very secluded. You don't know who to trust, especially the people you were already trusting. It eats away at your current relationships and causes you to avoid new ones. You aren't sure how to trust anyone ever again.

If you were like me at that point, you might not even be certain that you ever want to trust anyone again. When I was at this point, I became hyper- independent. I wouldn't allow myself to be dependent on anyone, ever, for anything; even when it was something that required interdependence. I created my own struggles from this and made my life harder than it had to be but for the sake of peace and safety and the illusion of control. I began to shut people out because in my head, if I didn't let anyone in then nobody could hurt me. If I didn't trust anybody, nobody could let me down. I think now looking back, I am not even sure I trusted myself. I had failed so many times to make good judgements of people that when I had succumbed to my last dagger, not only did I look like a pin cushion because I never learned to take my daggers out, but I was unsure of my ability to make the right choices so I just didn't make any. It was a very sad and very destructive way to live. I was on the edge of losing my closest friends, my business, my family, and my life. I didn't want to have to live like that and couldn't see any way out, so I thought I might just be better off dying. At least then I wouldn't hurt anymore. But that was just the confusion of betrayal, that little buoy that floated right on top to remind me of all the bad things that have hurt me.

It is time to start pulling out the daggers. Without doing this you cannot live, you cannot survive. I would not have survived if I hadn't started to pull out the daggers. Most daggers can be pulled out on your own if you're willing, and truthfully, it will more than likely hurt just as bad as when they went in. But some daggers you can't reach on your own, you are going to need help. You are going to have to trust someone enough to cause you pain in order to heal because pulling out a dagger does not feel good, but it is necessary. To pull them out on your own, you are going to have to reflect on those times and individually deal with each situation one at a time. It is not going to happen quickly. It took you years to get all those daggers. It might take you years to pull them out.

You will need to have healthy support nearby because it is going to hurt, and you're going to need to be encouraged to continue and that you are truly doing the right thing. Whoever stuck that dagger in you is no longer holding on to it. You were stabbed. It's past tense. That means it is done. You will need to learn how to move on from each and every situation because those situations are over. They are behind you. If you hold onto the past, it is going to blind you to the future. Yes, it hurt then, and it hurts now, but it is time to pull out that dagger and begin to heal.

You're most likely going to bleed; sometimes a little, sometimes a lot. If you have had a dagger for a long time, your body might have started to grow around it. You might have changed your entire lifestyle to accommodate your dagger, and now you're going to have to learn how to change it again.

Some of the daggers will require assistance. There are just some things that you are not going to be able to overcome on your own. You're going to have to learn how to trust again at some point, and let somebody help you. You are going to need to be vulnerable again because what you are trying to reach is just out of your grasp, and overreaching to do it on your own is only going to hurt more and make things worse. There are still trustworthy people. No matter how bad it got, no matter what happened, there will always be at least one person who will be trustworthy enough that you can give them a chance. They can reach your dagger; they can help you, but you're going to have to ask. It is not easy to ask for help, especially when you have been hurt so much by the ones who were always supposed to help you, always supposed to be there for you unconditionally.

Pulling the daggers out is so important. I would say that if you don't do this, and cannot do this, then you need to slow down. You're going to continue to struggle with every relationship. Every life situation that bumps your daggers is going to hurt you. You're not supposed to feel pain all the time. I spent far too many years leaving the daggers in; so long that it had affected every relationship and every aspect of my life. I operated on pain management. I had to assess every situation based on how much it would hurt and for how long. I couldn't develop good relationships when I was convinced that everybody was just going to hurt me eventually. I had to pull out the daggers other people used on me so I wasn't holding the last one that was used. I needed to heal, and I needed help. I had a lot of places in my life I couldn't reach on my own. I had to become vulnerable again. I had to trust people again.

I had to learn how to believe in myself and trust my own decisions once again. It wasn't easy. In fact, even as I write this book I am still healing from all those wounds and maybe still have some daggers to pull out. But this book is my healing bandage. I can sort through my thoughts, reflect on my past, and put it in a form that I can help others. It doesn't have to be a book; it could be a journal, a painting, or a quiet walk, but I would encourage you to find your own bandage to help you heal when you're ready to pull out the dagger.

Chapter 12:

THE LITTLE THINGS

I love getting favored attention, probably just as much as the next person. I am not someone that always wants or needs the spotlight. I don't always crave attention. I would be perfectly content to be in the background and quietly go about my business most of the time. I do enjoy the occasional spotlight, recognition for achievement or some other positive thing. I would be happier to receive favored attention than just attention itself. Favored attention is more personal. It is one-on-one recognition specifically designed to make you feel good about yourself because you deserve it. It isn't a spotlight for everyone else to see. It is a candle to hold in your corner. When public recognition becomes your goal, everything you do becomes a way to achieve that status, and you forget to focus on what matters. When you are more concerned with the results and recognition you are going to receive, you aren't spending time on the little things. You are not focusing on other people. More importantly, sometimes, on the other person. If you are focused on the big things, your actions can come across as selfish, or worse, they might actually be selfish.

Take in the moment when you get one, but don't forget how you got there. It is very likely that along the way, many people played a small role in either your support or your success. The little encouragements along the way: when you wanted to quit, they said something to keep you going; when you were down, they gave you a hug; when you were stuck, they helped you out. It's ok to be successful, it's ok to be great, it's ok to be wealthy. Don't get stuck on determining where other people are in comparison to you. Everybody has a story, and every story has a process. My story constantly felt like it was a few chapters behind everyone else's. I think now, when I consider all that I have tells a part of my story, I wasn't behind. I just have a longer story. I have many people who are a part of my story, even in a small way, that did little things for me but made a big difference.

The little things matter, probably even more than the big things. A computer has circuit boards filled with lots of tiny little things stored inside a relatively big thing. Our bodies are big things with skin and bones and organs, but every single one of those big things can be broken into very, very little things that, without them, we would not be able to function. Our DNA is a very little thing, and even just the slightest little change on that little level could cause incredibly dramatic changes.

When it comes to objects, it is easy to think about and see the little things and understand how they play a role in the big picture. But it might not be as easy to see how the little things can affect relationships.

The little things, when it comes to relationships, can be the determining factors of the health and success of those relationships. Starting in childhood, we get praised for doing something simple. People love to celebrate us as infants; the "firsts" of everything. When a baby opens their eyes, when they smile, the first time they make a sound, their first dirty diaper, their first yawn, their first sneeze; these are tiny little things that babies do, but we celebrate them with laughs and smiles every time. We encourage these things to be done, and they bring so much joy to both us and the babies. We reinforce to them through the celebration of these little things they do that we love them and care about them and that they are important.

As they grow into toddlers our celebrations are fewer, but still a lot of focus is on the firsts. The first time you know they recognize you, the first time they roll over, scoot, sit, crawl, walk, et cetera. We celebrate their first words, their childishly creative artwork, their laugh, and simply just how adorable they look. As they go through childhood, we commend them on learning to write their name and learn the alphabet. We encourage them in athletics and other activities.

Slowly but surely, all the focus we had on recognizing the little things melts into the praise of bigger and bigger things, and pretty soon, it is almost as if the little things no longer matter. It's like we outgrow the little things. Could you imagine the looks you would get as an adult if you just suddenly began praising and celebrating every time another adult spoke, sneezed, walked, or pretty much did anything? People would think you are ridiculous, but we still need personal favored attention even as adults.

Think about your close friends, the ones you most often spend time with or would prefer to spend your time with. How do they make you feel? You probably feel pretty good when you spend time together and after you part ways. I heard it said once that, "a friend is someone who, after you have spent time with them, you feel better about yourself". Are your friends people that make you feel better about yourself? Not because they put themselves down or because you didn't believe in yourself, but because they chose to focus on the little things that you do or the little things about you that make you who you are. They celebrate you for who you are, and you know that you are acknowledged and appreciated. They are your friends because you mutually celebrate each other and the little things you do in your relationships. When they focus on the little things in your life, you feel important, you feel like you matter because they give value to what you are and who you are.

Occasionally, you might find a friend who takes a particular interest in you and all the little things about you, even more than all your friends already do. That usually leads to a more intimate relationship, like a boyfriend or a girlfriend. This can be a difficult transition for some people because they are used to addressing the little things intermittently as you get together, but when you cross that line to a closer, more significant relationship, you often spend a lot more time together. Usually, when we start a new relationship like this, we treat the other person like an infant, and we progress similarly to the process we experienced growing up. We begin the relationship with an infatuation with the other person.

Everything they do is incredible and perfect, well worth the effort of celebration and recognition. Every time they smile, we feel the warm fuzzies. When we lock eyes, we become mesmerized and lost in the fantasy of possibility. When they sneeze, it's 'so cute'. When they have a silly quirk, it is fun to joke about and easily tolerable. We celebrate the first date, the first kiss, the first of everything. Some people even go so far as to celebrate the anniversary weeks and months after every seemingly significant event, overjoyed and ecstatic to be in a relationship and be a part of each other's lives.

Over time, we become closer and closer, developing special bonds that give us deeper rooted feelings and stronger connections. We fall in love, and at some point, some of us get married. That is where our "childhood relationship" ends for so many if it even lasted that long. So often, by the time we actually get married, we have already reached the teen years of recognition and are only celebrating the major things. For some of us, the major things feel less like celebration and more like condemnation. Our significant others forget to look at the little things we do well or that make us unique, and they begin to only acknowledge the big things we do well and focus on all the little things we do poorly. This causes a shift in the relationships we find ourselves in. They become less fun and more like work. It's as if now we have to try to love them rather than just being a fluid reaction to their very presence.

When you get into a routine, it can be difficult to recognize that what you're doing isn't the best thing for you because it is now familiar, instinctual muscle memory. Sometimes a routine is a bad thing, especially if your routine involves finding all the things your partner is doing wrong. If you stop and take a minute to assess your current significant relationship, what do you find? Are you nagging about little things or praising little things? Are you dreading going home because you don't get any attention, or are you excited to be there because your spouse intentionally notices you? I know everybody has a different 'love language', and I believe it is very important for each spouse to understand how to communicate in the other's language, but be sure to pay attention to the little things. If your husband comes home from work, what's the first thing you say? Is it pleasant? Are you genuinely interested in his day?

Are you excited with him for the things he is excited about? Maybe he accomplished something small but significant to him, and you should be celebrating that with him. The little things matter. Do you run your hand across his back as you pass by him, run your fingers through his hair when he is sitting next to you, or give him that cutesy smile from across the room? Find out what little things make him feel important, what makes him feel acknowledged, and what makes him feel loved.

Husbands this one is for you. Do you pay attention to the little things your wife does or says? Do you call her randomly in the middle of the day to tell her you miss her or that you love her? Do you bring her flowers on just the cliché holidays, or when you're in trouble; or do you do it on days she isn't expecting when your only reason for gifting them is to show her you're thinking of her? When you come home from work, are you setting big expectations, or are you appreciating the little things, like the fact that she is smiling at you when you walk in the door or that she made your favorite dinner because she knows you had a hard day? Do you acknowledge the fact that maybe she isn't feeling well, but she is still trying to show you attention? Talk to her, ask her about *her* day, and talk about the little things that are important to her. She has emotional needs, too. If you just do the little things every day, it will make a dramatically big difference.

Your relationship is alive. The DNA of your relationship is so sensitive that you need to be careful to pay attention to the little things along the way so you don't end up with a deformed monster for a relationship. When you focus on the little things, and you are able to celebrate what everyone else considers insignificant, you will be so much more excited to celebrate and appreciate the big things when they happen. Because, without all those little things along the way, the big things wouldn't have been possible. Don't leave room for the little negative things because when a lot of little negative things happen along the way, big negative things result from it. When a lot of positive little things happen along the way, big positive things happen. Big things are great; celebrate them, acknowledge them, remember them, but cherish the little things because they go as quickly as they come, and each one is unique in its own way.

Chapter 13:

ENTREPRE "NEWER"

Being an entrepreneur is not just owning a business. It is a way of thinking, a way of living. Anybody can buy or start a business if they have enough money, but successfully operating that business or coming up with the idea in the first place is entrepreneurial. It is a thought process of creating new products, services, applications, etc. It is the thought process not to reinvent the wheel because the wheel already works, but instead to come up with something else the wheel can do that nobody else thought of. Being an entrepreneur is the ultimate "open-mindedness", where every idea is worth pursuing; there's always room for improvement, and there is no such thing as impossible, only a solution you have not yet tried. Being an entrepreneur allows a certain level of freedom and control, at least perceived, over working at a "job" and pursuing someone else's dream.

There are, of course, added risks that you must be willing to take, many unknowns, and no real promise that what you do is good or right or that it will even work. Sometimes having a job and working toward someone else's dreams and goals for them is much safer and much more secure. There is not anything wrong with having a job, and there is nothing wrong with being an entrepreneur. Sometimes, someone can implement their entrepreneurial process into their job, and they are much more effective, much more valuable, and they are happy because they are heard and feel valued.

I grew up working on the farm, well, a farm. I had the simple task of cleaning horse stalls, sweeping floors, and other general mindless cleaning tasks. It was very repetitive and not very exciting. I had about 50 stalls to clean and two very long rows of barn aisles to sweep and keep clean twice a day. I remember having to get inside the stalls with the horses, and the sour smell would sometimes be so overwhelming from the concentration of ammonia in the pile of horse urine and pine shavings that my nose and eyes would burn. Some of the horses were a bit jumpy and unpredictable. I never knew if I was going to be kicked, shoved into a wall, or just completely ignored. I had to be constantly aware of every move they made and where I was standing in case I needed to make a quick exit. It was mundane work and 99% of the day I was alone, nobody to talk to during my day, no music to pass the time; just me, a rake, and a wheelbarrow.

I would watch the tractor driving around outside and wish I could be doing that instead of shoveling manure. I wanted more, to move up, to do something different. Eventually, as I spent months and years working there, I was given additional tasks, promoted in a way. I did eventually get to drive the tractors, ATVs, farm trucks, pick up supplies, and so on. I was given more responsibility and more freedom, but I was still working alone. There was nobody to share the workload with and nobody to hold me accountable for the task at hand.

I was given very wide boundaries, and I even felt at times I didn't have boundaries. I could come and go as I pleased and my only responsibility was to make sure the job was done. It didn't even matter how I did it as long as it was completed. This, I believe, awoke the entrepreneur in me. Even though I was helping someone else pursue their dreams and goals, I was developing the thought process and work habits that I would later use in my own life and business.

I learned how to think about different ways to complete a project and practice trial and error while learning to stick it out even if the project was difficult. I had to put up barbed wire and cattle panel fencing on my own. Thousands of feet of fencing, by myself. It was problem-solving and work ethic development at its finest. I was given the space and opportunity I needed to believe that anything was possible if I tried enough ways, enough times, and never quit until it was finished.

I remember starting a "normal" job and working for a company rather than a farm and working around people and structure. I enjoyed the people and sometimes the company, but the structure felt limiting and controlling. I definitely did not feel freedom. I was excited to start something new every time I started a new job, but I quickly became frustrated with the structure. Somebody else was in control, and I was just supposed to do things in a specific way at a specific time, even if there was a better way to do it. I was allowed a break only when they said, I was allowed to eat only when they said, I was allowed to go to the bathroom only when it was convenient for them, and I was only allowed to have time off or leave when and if they said it was ok. I felt like a slave to someone else's agenda. I wanted to travel, I wanted to take the day off, I wanted to stay home sick, I wanted to spend time with my family, but I needed to work. I needed something different, but the security of having a regular paycheck was too comforting. I didn't have a way out so I felt stuck, and because I felt stuck, I was unhappy.

It was because of these reasons, and a few more, that I chose to step out and begin my own company. I needed freedom, I needed options, I needed control of my life. It was definitely a major risk, with the potential for a great reward, but no guarantees. I was very excited to be stepping out on my own and chasing my own dreams and goals, but once I began I realized I was in uncharted territory. I had no idea where to start. Where do I get work? How do I find customers? Who pays me? How much do I make? When do I get paid? Where do I get supplies? The questions went on and on, and I didn't have the answers. I needed help. I needed somebody who had done this before to show me some things that work, to teach me some mistakes to avoid, somebody who had been where I was and where I wanted to be.

The business did well and I was able to grow and achieve the goals I set out for, as well as goals I didn't expect. Goals like receiving awards for my work and being invited to work for people and places I never thought possible. I started other businesses and even helped others start and grow businesses of their own. I was helping people achieve freedom, control, and the pursuit of their dreams. I was able to try new things and come up with new solutions to old problems. I was creative in ways that I hadn't had the opportunity to be before.

I learned to manage people and teach others to work together toward a common goal. I became the "they" that I had fought so hard to escape, but there were people out there who needed the "they" because they enjoyed the comfort of security, and that's ok. But since this book is not about business, let's move on and apply these ideas to relationships.

Relationships are exciting; at least, they are in the beginning. When a new relationship begins, it is new. It is fresh; there are so many unknowns about it. I am not just talking about a boyfriend or a girlfriend. That is almost always exciting even if just for a little while. When a new baby is born, we get excited about that new relationship. When we make a new friend, we get excited about the possibilities. A new relationship can be a crossroads where you choose the "job" or the "entrepreneur" path. If you treat it like a job, you are essentially giving the other person control of your life. You allow them to make decisions for you and set up your boundaries. They give you your structure of rules to follow in the relationship. You become dependent on them and sometimes that feels ok, sometimes you feel trapped.

Suppose you choose a "job" relationship. In that case, you might be looking for the security of the other person making all the decisions for you. You put the other person in a position of such authority in your life that you no longer have to make decisions and you, in your own mind, relieve yourself of any responsibility. The problem is that a real healthy relationship is a two-way street. If you allow a one-way street to develop, you are creating an opportunity for a controlling relationship. This could be a friend, a boyfriend/girlfriend, or even a child. As a parent, if you allow your children to set boundaries and make your relationship structure, you put them in control. I know a parent/child relationship is a little different than other relationships, but at the same time, you're still allowing control to be one-sided. Children don't have the experience to create the correct, healthy boundaries. They don't understand responsibility and consequences, and they haven't "been there" before.

It is like a new entrepreneur buying a big business they've never experienced and making the rules. They have no idea how anything works, they have no understanding of the process, and they are doomed from the start. Suppose you let your children set the relationship up. In that case, you will struggle with them showing you respect, and you will lack reasonable influence in their life. It is unhealthy for them and unrealistic as an example for other relationships they will experience in their life.

You almost need to teach your children through the "job" structure how to awaken their "entrepreneurial" selves in relationships. They need the comfort and security of learning from someone who has already been there so that when they are ready, they can step out on their own to form their own healthy relationships and be successful in them.

When you make new friends, you have equality. You both found something in common with each other and became friends because you were on level ground. If you give control to the other person, either all at once or slowly over time, you are creating unhealthy friendships. You might think it is ok because it feels comfortable, and you have little risk, but you're actually setting yourself up for struggle. When someone else has control of your friendship, you become dependent on them, and not in a good way. You might be more accepting of bad habits or even low levels of abuse just to stay in your "comfort zone". Over time, those small habits grow into bigger habits and are possibly more damaging. You become more and more accepting of them because the normal continues to advance based on your acceptance of your current circumstances.

You begin to allow the friend to call the shots. They tell you when you're going to hang out and where you're going to get together. They might be offensive to you in public or even put you down, but you stay around and brush it off for the security of your "job" relationship.

If you allow yourself to be abused and controlled, you're sending a message to yourself that it is ok to be treated this way. You are lowering your own standards and allowing somebody else to tell your worth to you. You need to know your value and your worth based on truth and fact, not somebody else's actions toward you. If your friendship is one-sided and you don't have control, you need to wake up and see it for what it is. I am not saying that you cannot be friends with this person anymore, but at the very least, you should re-evaluate your role and your boundaries in the friendship.

It is ok to have a conversation with that person and let them know how you feel. It is important to remember that it is not entirely their fault and not entirely your fault. You both have played a role in the development of that relationship. If you find this to be a common theme in all your friendships, then maybe it is time to talk to somebody about the way you develop relationships. Consider a therapist a "job coach", somebody that is going to help you be more effective and achieve the goals you set out to achieve. You are going to be happier with yourself and your relationships if you feel like there is some equal level of control in your life.

When you start dating someone, there is always excitement. If not, why would you start dating? This is someone new, something you've never experienced before, with infinite possibilities of things to come. In a way, you might be comfortable in a certain role in a dating relationship. Maybe you naturally like to take control, and perhaps you like to give up that control from the start. Suppose you give up control and freedom at the beginning of the relationship. In that case, nothing is your fault, and everything is their fault. You feel in control by giving up control.

If you take control, then everything is up to you, but only you, making the other person lesser than you in your subconscious mind. It is almost like a manager/employee relationship from the start, and that is not healthy. To put it in simple terms, you need to be coworkers hired at the same time, working together toward a common goal. When one person takes control or the other simply just gives it up, they have again created the opportunity for unhealthy dependency. It is ok to feel attached to somebody, especially if you're going to marry them or are already married, but it is not ok to need them in a way that you can't function without them telling you how to function, when to function, and where to function.

Controlling relationships usually develop over time and can be difficult to recognize from the inside. It is similar to boiling a frog. If you raise the temperature of a pot of water a little bit at a time, the frog doesn't realize it is being cooked alive until it's too late. A woman can be accepting of a man abusing her in small increments, maybe calling her a name or talking down to her. If she allows this, the temperature goes up. Then, he might push her or start yelling at her. Again, if this is allowed and overlooked, he is given control over her boundaries, and the temperature rises.

Eventually, if she doesn't jump out of the pot, the water boils, the man severely hurts her or even kills her, or she takes her own life. Feeling trapped, like there's no escape, she doesn't reach out for help and gives up her freedom for her perceived security of being in a relationship rather than being alone. She keeps working at her terrible job rather than being unemployed.

The same is true in the other direction. A man can be abused slowly by a woman and end up in the same place. At first, she begins by complaining, but that leads to condescension and belittling. It might start in private but then escalate to public humiliation. He accepts it a little bit at a time because the temperature is slowly turned up. Eventually, she might become physical toward him and even make wild, false accusations. The man slowly boils to death and takes his own life out of shame or remains miserable out of his own stubbornness.

What does an "entrepreneurial" relationship look like? Well first, you must be willing to take risks, but smart risks. Suppose your relationships look like any of those mentioned earlier. In that case, you might need to consider "quitting your job" and starting a new one or stepping out into a "new business". As I stated at the beginning of the chapter, entrepreneurial-minded individuals have a different way of thinking. In a relationship, it is important to be open-minded. You should not forget that you are in fact, two different people with two different ideas for every situation. You're not always right, and they're not always wrong.

Sometimes you're both right, and both ways of doing something are good and effective. There are no impossible tasks, only solutions you have yet to find. If you don't agree with the other person, or the circumstances of disagreement are seemingly impossible, use an open-minded process to come up with new ways to approach the situation. There will be times when you are in uncharted territory, and you need to get the advice and expertise of somebody who has been there before.

It is ok to need help; it is even more ok to ask for help. A successful entrepreneur knows when to get help, the same way a successful relationship thrives under the guidance of someone who can offer solutions to things you're facing that they have overcome.

A relationship that is healthy and entrepreneurial will be exciting every day. You never know what is going to happen, but because you're focused on success and constantly open-minded to new ideas, you anticipate only something better for you inside your relationship. Inside your relationship! As in, inside your business. You wouldn't be running a business and going to work for the competitor, so don't live your relationship with one person looking for another. You are working on your business, on your relationship. Don't start a "side hustle" because you're not getting everything you want in your business. If you are unhappy or not completely satisfied with your relationship, work on it from the inside. You have a partner, and a partnership is bigger than just your needs. Open up communication and be accepting of other ideas that might not be your own, because that is how healthy relationships grow. The moment you step out of your relationship and into the competitor's business, you might as well close up shop. You need to make a decision to stay committed to the process and the person.

When you treat your relationship like your own business, in partnership with your significant other, you have the opportunity for endless success and growth. You can chase your dreams together and accomplish everything you set out to do, even develop and discover dreams you never knew you had. If you're successful in your relationship, you can help teach others the steps and process to be successful as well.

Investing your time together to help other people will strengthen your relationship and give you common goals. Share your new ideas with each other, talk about new ways to use the wheel, and be open-minded to hear the other side of the story. When you put together a successful business it takes time, sacrifice, and humility. When you put together a healthy relationship, the same ingredients are necessary. Be willing to put in the time, be patient, understand you're going to have to make some sacrifices and be humble. It is ok to seek out help from somebody who has been where you are or where you want to go. You don't know everything; you're not always right, and they're not always wrong, but together, you can find a solution that works.

Chapter 14:

LIVING BEYOND THE MOMENT

It would not be easy to think that anybody goes through life without ever thinking about the future. But how much do you really think about who you are and how what you do will affect the generations that come after you?

When you go to school, when you go to work, when you raise a family, when you make decisions while you're alone, hurt, angry, or how you decide to treat other people. Every one of these things can have lasting effects, but if you are not considering anything beyond right now at this moment, you might not realize that you are making potentially terrible mistakes. The opposite could also be true, that you might be doing great things, but you just don't realize it.

When you approach any of your life's situations, take a moment to think long-term. You certainly need to be conscious in and of the moment, but if you are able to also consider how the next moments will shape the future of people who might not even exist yet, you begin the process of leaving your own legacy. You might make the world a better place, but it might not happen until long after you are gone. It might be because of something small you did or didn't do, that caused a change in somebody that also made a choice with or for someone else that you will never know. You can be great now, and that can last generations.

Some relationships are dangerous or toxic. Those relationships can affect your other relationships. If you have a child and the other parent makes your skin crawl, your first reaction might be to teach the child about the other parent's flaws. You might want to tell them all about how to have a broken relationship with that other parent. But that is not good, and that lasts longer than you will be around. You need to understand that both the good things and bad things have lasting effects. Suppose you choose to teach that child to love, respect, and to honor everybody. In that case, you are leaving a long-lasting effect that encourages that child to respond differently toward someone of similar character later in their own life.

When you go to work, do you just do enough to not get fired? What if you went above and beyond because you know that something you do now will affect somebody later? Maybe it will be a result of the hard work or dedication you portrayed that helped shape the face of your company, shape future policies, and create the steps for new breakthroughs after you are gone. I would much rather be a part of the positive results and direction of my past employers than the ruin and destruction of them. Something you do now could create an opportunity for someone else to do something great. Don't take away the value that you present to the current times because you don't understand something you will never see. Take pride in your work. Even the simplest of jobs are important and have their place in the efforts of advancing society.

Your habits determine your character. What you do when people are watching isn't always as important as when they're not. You have to have a certain amount of integrity when you are alone, a certain amount of self-control, and a certain amount of discipline. These choices will affect the way you perceive yourself, even if nobody else will ever know. You know what you do and who you are, and these decisions can affect not only you but the people around you. They might become trapped by your choices or ideals and suffer the same silent consequence of self-destruction. Your suffering could result in self-harm, which most certainly will affect generations to come. Your decisions could also be equally reinforcing, causing you to pass along a quiet strength to generations to come.

You could have developed incredible individual qualities when you are alone that can be passed down and help others to become better, stronger, and healthier people. Your choices could cause incredible self-awareness and self-confidence that make you, and anyone who learns from you, resilient to the things that they encounter in life. It could be just what someone needs to hang on a little longer. You could be passing down hope through generations.

Relationships are multi-dimensional and have a lasting effect on people and relationships yet to come. What you do now matters today, and it matters tomorrow. There are so many ways to grow in your ability to develop relationships with everyone in your life. You need to learn to cater to the type of relationship you want and understand the needs of the other person you are having a relationship with. You get to set up the future with the decisions you are making now, and that is an incredible responsibility. Learn to think bigger than yourself, understanding that being selfless is not a weakness but rather a sign of strength. You do not need to focus on yourself because you already know who you are and how you fit into your place in each of your relationships.

You now have the opportunity to influence others who are still on the journey of discovering themselves and learning how to have relationships with you because you have put in the work to set the example. It is never too late to start working on yourself. When you do something today, make it last, make it matter, and make it your legacy. Whatever is going on in your moment, you have a decision. You can live in the moment, or you can live beyond the moment.

Chapter 15:

THIS IS ME

There is only one version of you, and that is who you are right now. You are unique in your own way and you are your own individual person with incredible qualities. You are awesome. Embrace what makes you special. You ought to be proud of who you are because if you don't like yourself, how can you expect anyone else to? Once you have discovered your true identity, live that out in your life everyday. Become better and better at being you. Not everybody is going to "arrive" at the same time. We all have our battles, our journeys, and our unique life lessons but, ultimately, our goal should be the same; to be the best self we can be.

Understanding that we are all unique individuals with our own stories and our own experiences should help us to manage our relationships in a more healthy.

You have taken a look at yourself now and realized that maybe there are some things you can work on, so keep in mind that everyone around you might be at any infinite number of points in that process, if they have even started at all. Not everybody is as ambitious as you. Not everybody wants to change or even think they have anything to change.

If you understand yourself you are better able to relate to others, even if they're difficult people. It is important to allow people room to be themselves and discover themselves. As you go through your own process and learn to be better, you most likely have some ugly flaws and difficult characteristics, but you hope that you are accepted as who you are at that time. It feels good to be accepted where you're at, especially when you know where you're going.

You don't need to walk around with a chip on your shoulder or with overwhelming arrogance. Strong confidence is enough to propel you through your process and on to the next step. Be proud that you are who you are, even if you have made mistakes. Just be willing to learn from those mistakes so that you don't have to keep reliving them. What you have done in the past, every single choice, every action, every thought, every experience, has made you exactly who you are right now at this very moment. Don't discredit yourself for not being where you would like to be or where you think you should be based on someone else's standards. Know and understand your past, good or bad, and use that to shape your future self. Use it as an education to ensure you either are or become someone that you can be proud of.

You need to understand that not everybody is going to like you or agree with you; that's what makes loving yourself so great. Nobody should ever have a greater impact on your self-image than you. I don't know what your beliefs are, but I believe Jesus was a completely perfect person without any faults whatsoever. He loved everybody. He healed people and brought people back from the dead. He created miracles and people still talk about all those things today.

Despite these things, there were still people who didn't like him; in fact, they killed him because they hated him. So maybe you need to lower your expectations because nobody is perfect; and if the only one who was perfect still wasn't universally loved and adored, why would you expect any different? It isn't that you're not valuable or not worth loving, it's just that some people see things differently than you, and that is completely okay. You still need to learn to co-exist because killing each other is no longer an acceptable form of dealing with misaligned points of view.

When you walk through life, your attitude should be "This is me". Not in the way that you are cramming it down somebody's throat, but in the way that you are proud to be who you are and even more proud about who you are becoming. If you can accept yourself with all your faults, flaws, and failures, then you begin to learn to accept others through all of theirs. Don't forget to acknowledge and appreciate your own successes and victories either, no matter how small they may seem. This will help you recognize it in others as well, making you more pleasant to be around and creating deeper relationships with everyone in your life. It is important to lift each other up, but it starts with ourselves. Be you, be proud of being you, and keep being you. Nobody else can even come close to being as awesome as you are when you just be yourself.